WHEN

WOMEN

TALK

WHEN
WOMEN
TALK

10 INFLUENTIAL WOMEN
SHARE STORIES OF LEARNING,
LIFE, AND LEADERSHIP

CURATED BY CATHY KUZEL

Published by

North Vancouver, British Columbia, Canada
WhenWomenTalk.ca

Cover and text design by Carly Franklin, BOOST Design + Marketing
Copy-editing and proofreading by Naomi Pauls, Paper Trail Publishing

Cataloguing-in-Publication data

Kuzel, Cathy, editor.
When women talk : 10 influential women share stories of life, learning, and leadership / Cathy Kuzel.
North Vancouver, BC: The Connected Woman, 2023.
ISBN: 978-1-7380791-0-0 (paperback)
LCSH Women—Biography. | Women executives—Biography. | Entrepreneurship. | Leadership in women. | Businesswoman—Biography. | Success in business. | BISAC BIOGRAPHY & AUTOBIOGRAPHY / Women | BIOGRAPHY & AUTOBIOGRAPHY / Business | BUSINESS & ECONOMICS / Entrepreneurship | BUSINESS & ECONOMICS / Motivational
LCC HD6054.3 .W44 2023 | DDC 658.4/092—dc23

For those who have blazed a trail for us to follow.

CONTENTS

DEAR READER

"Save me!" If only the hardest thing I had to do was write an incredible introduction to this book. Computer crashes, chapter deadlines, overdue invoices (mostly receivable), family dramas ... the list goes on. There are times in my life when I wish a smart collie would race back to the farm to tell someone I've fallen down the well so they can pull me to safety. Or that a masked man would appear out of nowhere on his white horse to drive away those "bad people" who are making my life miserable. Or maybe, someone of noble blood would whisk me away from my daily trials and tribulations. Unfortunately, those kinds of dramatic rescues only happen in the movies.

Fact is, life happens, and we have a starring role in it but no one ever told us that the script may change at a moment's notice. *And* they neglected to tell us that should that script no longer work for us, we could choose a new storyline. Only after operating within the status quo for a number of years did I finally realize I could write a new storyline for conducting business.

In 2008, I created The Connected Woman® community in Vancouver, British Columbia, Canada, because I was done with the prevailing script in business. I wanted to bring the personal connection back to the professional arena—to provide a space in which women could share with and learn from other women. The intention was to converse, collaborate, and create. This book, published to mark The Connected Woman's fifteenth anniversary, is an extension of that vision.

When Women Talk is a collection of stories from ten remarkable women, giving you the insight and motivation to muster the courage to write your own script. You'll read about women who have overcome adversity and broken through barriers to achieve great success in their personal and professional lives. Don't you just love those kinds of endings?

The authors share real-life situations from life and business with tools for making your voice heard, gaining respect, and creating opportunities to shape your career, provide for your family, and, along the way, make our world a better place to live. The stories inside this book will remind you that no matter how hard a situation becomes, you are not alone, and you too can find solutions and overcome obstacles to create a different outcome.

Just as in the movies, we all face challenges throughout our life and careers that can threaten to overwhelm us. If you're looking for inspiration and practical advice on how to navigate change and embrace new opportunities, you'll find many "aha" moments in these pages. And one last thing . . . When you read about a clever idea or discover a resource within the following pages, share it with another woman. Let's create a community in which every woman is valued and respected, and works together with others in a meaningful way.

What steps will you take today to write your own script? Whom will you reach out to and lend a helping hand? How will you make this world a better place in which to live?

Cathy

Alone we can do so little; together we can do so much.—Helen Keller

CONNECTIONS COUNT
BY CATHY KUZEL

Talent, drive, confidence, creativity, and ambition are great qualities for an entrepreneur, but they alone are not enough. Success does not occur in a vacuum. Good relationships and connections are required.

AT THE AGE OF NINETEEN, I moved into a bachelor apartment, while working a part-time job to pay my expenses so I could continue my studies in music at the University of British Columbia. After I had unpacked and settled in, I went out to fill my pantry at the local grocery store. When I got to the checkout with my purchases, I wrote a cheque to pay for them, but the cashier refused to accept it without more identification than I had. My embarrassment grew as the store manager was called and proceeded to berate me in front of other customers, accusing me of being a student whose cheque would bounce.

I could have mirrored his anger and walked out without the groceries, but I decided to make a new friend instead. I apologized for the trouble I had caused and offered to get cash, since my bank was across the street. I returned with cash in hand, thanked the staff for keeping my groceries to the side until I returned, and bid them all a good afternoon. After that, each time I went into the store, I made an effort to learn names and have conversations, so not only was I becoming familiar with the staff but they were also getting to know me. They told me about their personal lives, and I shared mine. Eventually, the store manager gave me his card so I would not encounter the same problem again.

From that experience and others like it, I learned that sometimes you have to take the initiative and step forward with your hand extended. I learned how important it is to build relationships with people who can help you succeed. Talent, drive, confidence, creativity, and ambition are great qualities for an entrepreneur, but they alone are not enough. Success does not occur in a vacuum. Good relationships and connections are required.

No one succeeds alone

In 1990, when I started my first business as an independent sales representative for a fashion company, some people in my life were quick to warn me about the perils of a commission-based business. Despite the negative feedback, I had done my due diligence by researching the company through reports, online stats, and my connections. I focused on the company's business plan and growth potential and, most importantly, I believed in myself.

I shared my new business with my immediate connections, including friends and family, and soon found that other women wanted what I had. I began to build what would turn out to be an extremely successful nineteen-year career providing fashionable and affordable clothing to women across Canada. I attribute my success to the talented, driven, confident, creative, and ambitious women I surrounded myself with. Without them, I would not have achieved my goals.

It is crucial to build connections and relationships with people who can help you succeed. With the right people around you, nothing can stop you from achieving your goals. No one succeeds alone.

Building genuine connections

When it comes to expanding your network and making new friends, Dale Carnegie said it best: "You can make more friends in two months by becoming interested in other people than you can in two years by trying to get other people interested in you." This rings true in both personal and professional settings.

I experienced this principle first-hand while building my first business. Looking for a way to connect with more women outside of my immediate group of friends and acquaintances, I came across an announcement for a local women's networking group in the community event listings. I decided to attend, hoping to expand my customer reach and circle of influence.

By taking time to genuinely connect with others, showing appreciation for their contributions, and fostering a supportive environment, we can all thrive and build meaningful relationships both personally and professionally.

When I arrived at the meeting, I discovered that the group was quite small, and the women seemed unsure of how to present themselves and promote their businesses effectively. Something needed to change, I realized. I chose to speak up and offer my assistance to the organizer. Together, we revamped the group by rebranding it as SWAN: Successful Women Always Network. I designed a logo, established bylaws, hired a website builder, and as president, I set an ambitious plan to grow our network to a hundred members within two years.

My primary goal was to create a supportive and inclusive environment where women could comfortably develop their business skills and connect with like-minded individuals. It was crucial to recognize the expertise of every member, regardless of the type of enterprise they ran or their experience level. To break the ice at each meeting, we implemented a greeter program, ensuring that every guest received a warm welcome, assistance with registration, and an introduction to a member. As president, I followed up with each guest after every meeting, sending a handwritten note expressing gratitude for their participation and extending an invitation to join us as a member. Alternatively, I would send a monthly newsletter, reiterating the same message and inviting them back. Through these intentional efforts, we started to make genuine connections, and in less than two years, our network grew to surpass the hundred-member mark.

Throughout this journey, I learned a valuable lesson: just as I thrive on sincere recognition and appreciation, so do others. People inherently desire to be respected and valued for their contributions. They want to be seen as individuals and to feel a sense of belonging. Appreciation, in its various forms, fulfills a fundamental human need. When individuals receive recognition for their hard work, they feel valued. This, in turn, boosts their productivity and motivates them to continue to excel or to improve on what they have already achieved. It is truly amazing to witness the power of appreciation in action.

By taking the time to genuinely connect with others, showing appreciation for their contributions and fostering a supportive environment, we can all thrive and build meaningful relationships both personally and professionally.

Connections count

Sometimes, life has a way of changing your perspective. My mother-in-law was diagnosed with terminal cancer after I had been leading this successful network for eight years. Faced with a difficult choice between my family and my business, I saw that the decision was clear—I needed to step back from the network and other commitments to be there for my family.

During this challenging time, I relied on the business relationships I had built over the years to ensure things continued to run smoothly while I took a step back. However, this support was not limited to just business matters. I had to manage various tasks such as palliative care, legal and financial matters, and ultimately funeral arrangements. All of this, because it was an emotional time for our family, was an overwhelming experience, but with thanks I reached out to my connections for assistance.

I strongly believe that when women establish meaningful connections, these links can yield powerful results, rooted in helping others. By constantly thinking about how we can assist everyone we encounter—from the barista who prepares our morning coffee to the top authority in our industry—we open ourselves up to a world of possibilities and opportunities.

I cannot emphasize enough the importance of treating our connections, relationships, and the people in our circle of influence as a valuable asset. Just like a bank account, we need to make deposits in order to make withdrawals. Facing my mother-in-law's terminal illness was the first time I found myself in a position where I had to take instead of give, and it made me realize the number of people who considered me a friend and colleague.

A collaborative community

Coffee with Cathy™ emerged as a solution when I found myself constantly receiving requests from women wanting to meet over coffee. I have always believed in the power of shared knowledge, and I was eager to connect and share my experiences with other women. However, meeting one-on-one was taking up too much time.

To address this, I came up with the idea of organizing monthly group meetings. Instead of individual coffee dates, I would bring together four or five women to discuss topics relevant to their businesses. Not only did this allow me to connect with more women, but it also helped me to use my time more efficiently. I quickly saw that this format met a need, as more and more women expressed interest in attending these group coffee meetings. It was from this concept that The Connected Woman was born.

In my search for a women's organization that focused on exchanging ideas and empowering one another both professionally and personally, I couldn't find something that matched my vision. So I decided to create it myself. I wanted to move away from the traditional networking groups and events, where there was pressure to sell or pitch something in a brief time frame. I envisioned a community that emphasized collaboration and knowledge sharing, welcomed conversation, and provided a supportive space where women could learn and grow together. I proceeded to find out if others wanted the same thing.

I began by asking women what they expected in a networking group and what they had experienced. The compelling response was that they desired a sense of belonging to a community of like-minded women who understood the challenges of being in business. They wanted to connect, have meaningful conversations, collaborate, and create something to be proud of. These conversations helped shape the design and structure of The Connected Woman, which became a platform for women to exchange ideas, share experiences, offer solutions, and support one another.

> *We all have a purpose and a story to tell; there is someone who needs to hear it, and by showing up we can make a difference in someone's life, career, or business.*

In 2008 The Connected Woman was launched, and today it boasts a community of over three thousand women. It provides an online platform for personal and professional growth and fosters strong connections through online and local in-person events. Our networking model encourages women to go "Beyond the Business Card"® and form genuine alliances. By surrounding yourself with the right type of people—such as mentors, partners, and business advisors—you can increase your ability to succeed. You're as strong as the people with whom you associate.

If you want change, be the change-maker

Nothing happens until someone has initiative and takes action. Are there challenging issues that still need to be addressed in business and in society? Absolutely. Are there inadequacies and intolerances? Yes, and while a single voice can make an impact, many voices can make change. I encourage you to step forward, speak out, and show up.

- *Stepping forward* fosters a collaborative culture based on openness, trust, and realizing everyone's potential. If created with intention, such a culture encourages women to trust their ability and share their gifts in pursuit of a common goal. Rather than having to learn from our own mistakes or successes, we can reach out to the community and ask if anyone has had an experience that could assist us. Others have "been there, done that." Stepping forward, they can share their knowledge and experience, allowing us to learn from their mistakes and successes.

- *Speaking out* includes advocating, validating, commiserating, and cheerleading. Unless a need or thought is vocalized, we cannot read another person's mind. So we need to speak out when we need help or when we want change; speak out when someone needs encouragement or validation; speak out for someone who cannot speak for themselves.

Sometimes all we need is the knowledge that someone's got our back.

- *Showing up* inspires everyone, including ourselves. We can benefit when we surround ourselves with values-driven women who have a positive view and are focused on changing the world for the better. In strong communities there is always someone showing up, doing something amazing, which can inspire us to put in that extra effort and achieve bigger goals. We all have a purpose and a story to tell; there is someone who needs to hear it, and by showing up we can make a difference in someone's life, career, or business. Wisdom and insight become more valuable when shared.

Building personal connections and relationships is more important than ever in these digital times, with their sometimes-tenuous online links ("one click and I'm now your friend"). Lasting success has always been about quality, not quantity. While it's great to have thousands of follows, likes, and friends on your social media platforms, will those connections be there when you really need them, like mine were when I needed help?

Step forward and take small actions to invest in relationships, to create more positive connections with others around you, whether at the office, in the grocery store, on the bus, or in your neighbourhood. Speak out and acknowledge and appreciate the work of others. Recognize and celebrate successes—theirs and yours.

And always show up. Who you are is awesome and what you do makes a difference. Now go get connected!

CATHY KUZEL

A dynamic speaker, author, and award-winning business development expert with a deep knowledge of the art of human connections, Cathy is one connected woman. Through her coaching and consulting practice, Cathy finds great personal fulfillment in helping others succeed. She has developed and implemented strategic sales and marketing programs with proven success rates for small to mid-size companies by combining proven tools with focused coaching and "no excuses" accountability.

Cathy is a firm believer that "Knowledge shared is success magnified." She is also the founder of The Connected Woman, an organization supporting entrepreneurial women that encompasses diverse industries, levels of experience, and backgrounds: women who want to participate in a reciprocal process of exchanging knowledge, experience, and expertise—not just business cards.

Women who want to be "connectors," not "collectors."

The Connected Woman has a dynamic community model that allows women to build strong personal connections, resulting in even stronger business alliances—both offline and online. For more information, visit TheConnectedWoman.com.

- 🌐 CathyKuzel.com
- 🌐 TheConnectedWoman.com
- 🌐 WhenWomenTalk.ca
- 🌐 CSuiteLearningCenter.ca

WHY NOT ME?
BY JACQUIE McBAIN

What had I done? I had given up a six-figure income to be an entrepreneur. And now I would have to pivot. That is what you have to be able to do—adapt and find your strength.

DO YOU EVER PAUSE TO WONDER, *Why am I working for a company that doesn't appreciate what I do for them?* Do you wake up in the morning hating your job so much that you cry when you start your day? Maybe you've been passed over for an exciting new C-suite position. Was it because you were not a man? Have you ever tried to break through barriers into territory where no women have travelled before you and thought, *Why not me?* This is the story of my career.

Breaking barriers, hitting roadblocks

I didn't realize I would become a trailblazer and self-advocate when working at McDonald's at the young age of fifteen. In the 1970s, girls were hired to work the cash registers, wash the floors, and keep the restaurant clean. I thought, *Why couldn't I be in the back flipping the burgers?* My boss at the time laughed when I asked if I could get a shift making the hamburgers. "Why would you want to do that? You will get dirty and smell of grease!" My response was, "Why not me? Women cook in kitchens at home. Why not here?" To which there was at first no response, but as a result, I was the first girl to ever get a shift flipping burgers in the back, and I loved it!

I later took a job with a major bank, where there were only men as managers and women were tellers or secretaries. When asked during an employee annual review what were my aspirations, I said, "I want to be a manager of the department one day." The response was, "That takes hard work and dedication and, well, just keep on doing what you are doing and maybe one day that will happen." After a few years of taking as many courses as I could, I was given a supervisor role that had not been given to a female before.

A number of years on, after leaving banking, I entered the food industry, another male-dominated industry. And there I was, selling wieners, bacon, and ham. The buyers at the big grocery chains were all men, and I was the only female sales representative. Why I gravitated to these industries, I was not sure yet. My problem at this company was not the men, it was the other women employed there. Since I was confident, intelligent, and pretty, other women were threatened by me, even jealous, and decided that I was too successful and was making them look bad. They allied themselves like a pack of wolves and did everything they could to ensure I went through hell, so that I would quit.

This is when I learned I have more resilience and persistence than I ever thought was possible. Those women did not realize that *I don't back down.* After four years of this craziness, the company was acquired by another company back east. I was told I would not be needed anymore and the "guy" back east would take over sales for the West. I was heartbroken and in total disbelief. It didn't matter that I'd secured the company's first ever million-dollar order to Save-On-Foods. It didn't matter that the guy in the position before me didn't sell one item to Costco but that within one year I had six items on the shelves. A guy was going to assume my job! *Gosh, now what do I do?*

After a year of job searching, I got an account manager position in western Canada selling hardware and software solutions to the direct mail and printing industry. I was flown to California for training with fourteen others hired from all over North America. I should not have been shocked, but I sat down at the table with *all men*. The good news is the trainer was a female manager. *Great!* I thought. *Finally, a company that recognizes women in leadership roles.*

I was the first female salesperson to be hired in Canada. I won Rookie of the Year in my first year and went on to win several President Club trips. After ten years, of the fourteen men I had trained with, I was the only one still selling. Then, in 2015, I found out I would require brain surgery, a procedure that had never before been performed in the world. I was patient zero. After nine months of recovery, I was back in the saddle, to everyone's surprise—including my surgeons.

After a fifteen-year career, the company I worked for was sold to a venture capital company and, successful as I was, I was passed over yet again for an executive-level position filled by— you guessed it—a man. Once more I was looking for another job.

Career success despite the odds

After five interviews, I was successful in my search for employment and was hired by a software company selling to architects, engineers, and construction companies (AEC, in the business). Once again, I would be selling to lots of men. I just love a challenge! However, this proved to be the worst company I have ever worked for.

The company provided no leadership, poor communication, and eight weeks of largely unassisted training. No human interaction, no opportunity to ask questions; just eight weeks of seven-hour days watching technical videos and taking tests. Once I'd completed these, I attended three days at the self-proclaimed corporate "university." I was now armed with technical details, but no practical training. I was expected to field questions well outside the scope of training and told to ask my boss when needing assistance. I tried calling, texting, and e-mailing, but was seldom successful. Finally, I was able to ask, "What is your preferred communication method?" His response: "Text if it's urgent, e-mail if not." Annoyed, I replied, "Then why don't you answer my messages?" and he literally responded, "The phone gremlins must have eaten the messages." This went on for six months, with him never visiting me and never offering on-site client support, no matter the client size or importance.

The straw that broke the camel's back: I had set up an educational session with a large architectural firm, an international company with several offices around the world. I requested time on their calendar to have a subject expert make a presentation on our product solution(s). I did my job—I got time on the firm's agenda for two hours, two different sessions. I was told they would require in-person experts, not online presentations. I agreed and took this to my boss, who replied, "Terrific, no problem. Consider it done."

As the date got closer, I started to ask who was coming out to do the sessions but received no response. At last I heard back, "I will let you know in a few days." One week from the event, I received an e-mail telling me that no one could make the presentations and that I was going to have to do them—to thirty architects, engineers, and senior-level construction managers. I was *not* the subject expert; we had trained experts to do this job. I called my boss's boss, who said, "I had no idea you were able to get this type of opportunity with one of the largest firms in the world." He was going to help me, and he did. He found someone to fly in from Alabama for the first session, and the other would have to be an online presentation—not what the client had asked for, so they were not happy.

As this incident reveals, my boss was not a leader and certainly not a team supporter, which caused me untold grief. The crying started early on. I didn't want to get out of bed, and I absolutely hated my job. This was only three months in. I ended up aligning myself with other team members to compensate for the lack of support. Within a few months, my sales numbers were beating other reps (all men) in this division in western Canada. I was asked, "How are you selling in Vancouver territory that has been dead for ten years?" I responded, "I figured out how to work around my boss."

My success despite the lack of support made me think, *Why am I working my butt off for all of these companies, only to be disappointed, only to be frustrated? Why can't I be my own boss? How hard can that be?*

Surrounded by successful women entrepreneurs

For models of women who had achieved success in business, I did not have to look far. There were several within my own family. My mother worked at a bank for many years and was not happy with her job. She loved gardening and flowers, and one day she decided she wanted to own her own flower shop. To run her business, she worked long days and many weekends, especially during the special holidays. Her work ethic really inspired me.

Before Mother's Day, for example, she would be busy for weeks, to ensure she had sufficient inventory. When the calls for orders came in, she would be arranging flowers all day and into the wee hours. And even though it was Mother's Day, the store was open, so all moms would be happy. Unfortunately, my mom was so busy, there was no time for her to be celebrated as a mother. Her example taught me that there are sacrifices you make by being an entrepreneur. Hard work, dedication, and endurance are all prerequisites.

My younger sister had several great ideas for start-up companies and was way ahead of her time thirty years ago. She wondered how elderly people would get their groceries when they were unable to go in person to the grocery store. There was no delivery service in Winnipeg back then. She learned that many elders had family members, friends, or neighbours to assist them. But there were still those that had no one, so she started to deliver basics to a nice elderly man on a weekly basis. Shortly after she moved to the USA, after she got married. Our mom and stepfather carried on the deliveries, and when they travelled, I would take over. We continued this for ten years, until the senior passed. All these years later and even more so after the arrival of COVID-19, some grocery stores now deliver to your door and there are more services for people with disabilities.

My mother-in-law, another business mentor for me, owned a successful interior design store in White Rock, BC. I watched her work long hours, six days a week from morning till night. She sold custom drapes and blinds and custom furniture pieces along with beautiful interior decorating accessories, placing orders with several different suppliers. Huge cardboard boxes would arrive at the front door of her store, and my petite but very strong mother-in-law would have them opened and the contents put away in no time.

> *My mother-in-law gave me the best advice: "Whatever business you go into, make sure you can leverage the years of relationship building that you have done, as those people will be your first customers."*

One day in 2004, an unfortunate event occurred—a business owner's worst nightmare. In the middle of the night, the police called to say there was a fire in the bookstore right next door to her store. The firefighters had to break through her store to extinguish the fire from different angles. As she sat on the curb all alone, hearing the sound of broken glass and accessories being destroyed to try and save the building was just gut-wrenching. The next day when she returned to her store, she found *nothing* salvageable. The smoke damage was so bad that the entire space would need to be gutted and everything replaced.

Many people would have taken the insurance money and closed shop, but she did not. The daunting task of trying to rebuild her entire business and replace all the custom pieces would take many months. But her inner strength and dedication to her business, and to all of her clients, motivated her to rebuild. After a long nine months of hard work and sleepless nights, she reopened the store. Her clients came back in a big way; they truly supported her. Two years later, in 2006, she was able to retire and sold her successful business. I couldn't even imagine losing everything and starting again, but her resilience paid off. She was such a good role model, showing that perseverance can lead to a positive end result.

Besides the examples of my mother, sister, and my mother-in-law, I also have a sister-in-law who owns her own business. She started in sales, became an entrepreneur, and now runs one of the most successful interior design companies in Calgary. I have watched her over the years pour so much passion, sweat, and tears into this business, admiring and respecting her efforts. All these successful women surrounding me, so *why not me?*

Taking the plunge into promotions

I decided I wanted to get into the promotional business, offering swag or merch, as it is now referred to. I knew very little about this business, but thought, *Well, I can learn it.*

When I floated the idea of starting my own business, my daughters, now adults, who had watched how hard I have worked, turned out to be my biggest cheerleaders. My husband, who had stood beside me, watching the highs and lows over the years, said, "You got this!" My mother-in-law gave me the best advice: "Whatever business you go into, make sure you can leverage the years of relationship building that you have done, as those people will be your first customers."

In October 2018, I picked out a company name, Go To Promotions Inc., registered my business, wrote a business plan, and then set out to talk to the banks. After receiving several nos for funding, I finally got a yes from a credit union. My doors were open! I spent the next six months building my business and getting my name out there. Then everything came crashing to a halt in March 2020, due to COVID-19. Every time the phone rang, it was a client calling to postpone an event. Unfortunately, the public health guidelines at that time meant that the events were not postponed, they were all cancelled. Six months of hustle to get my company off the ground, and now *nothing*.

> *You never know how strong you really are until you realize your livelihood now depends on your strength to heal quickly and get back to work, because you have a company to run.*

What had I done? I had given up a six-figure income to be an entrepreneur. And now I would have to pivot. That is what you have to be able to do—adapt and find your strength. So I pivoted. I found out I could sell hand sanitizer and I could sell custom-printed face masks. My next move was to align myself with essential service companies. Construction companies, medical services, and banks were all open. I was starting to find my stride again.

Then bad news hit. I was told I needed to go for a second brain surgery. How was my company going to make it through this? I would need to be off work for six to nine months. *What now?* Luckily, one of my very best friends stepped out of retirement and said, "Train me. I will run the business for you until you are healthy enough to take it over again." With her and my husband on my side, we hired an administrative person and off for surgery I went. You never know how strong you really are until you realize your livelihood now depends on your strength to heal quickly and get back to work, because you have a company to run.

Go To Promotions has grown year over year, despite COVID, despite health challenges, but not without a lot of growing pains and challenges that have tested us. My first order was from winning a request for proposal (bid tender). I was literally jumping up and down with joy after getting my first big order—from a casino in Saskatchewan. Being new to the business, I didn't realize that my software database was not converted to Canadian dollars and that the pricing I had provided was in the higher US currency. So now I knew why I had won the tender. Mine was the cheapest bid, so cheap that I didn't make any money. My husband explained the situation best. "This was your university education tuition," he told me.

Plenty of people are full of talk, but the fact is, you don't know if you can do something until you try to do it. Yes, being in business for yourself is a tough road and a long road, with many twists and turns and small speed bumps. Sometimes the mountain you need to climb is so high, you don't think you will get to the top of it. But if you have the fight and the spirit in you, and are surrounded by supportive family and friends, why not try? Why not pave the path so that other women will say, "Hey, if she can do it, why not me?"

JACQUIE McBAIN

With years of exposure to an array of market-leading organizations, Jacquie has first-hand experience in how business changes from industry to industry as well as from year to year. For most of the past two decades, she has worked in the direct mail and printing sector, both as a solutions provider and an industry advocate. Her role has been to facilitate supplier marketing programs, business development initiatives, and partnership management.

Jacquie consolidated that knowledge and experience to launch her own company, Go To Promotions, in 2018. She has created a strong family business that incorporates those who are family by birth and those who are family by choice.

Her primary goal is to work with customers to find promotional products that will showcase their brand and in turn help in growing their business. Jacquie's brand purpose is to be Useful, Unique and Unforgettable and to help others do the same—in life and in business. In 2022 her company received a Business Excellence award for professional services from the Cloverdale District Chamber of Commerce.

- gotopromotionsinc.com
- @gotopromotionsinc
- mcbainjacquie
- @gotopromotionsinc

CHALLENGING OUR ASSUMPTIONS
BY LYNNE BRISDON

> *The evening sun was shining through the windows, casting kind of a magical spell. "I guess it would be fun to travel," I said, all the while having doubts about how we would be able to afford it. Making assumptions that it was not possible.*

HELPING PEOPLE START BUSINESSES as a business coach and now managing the Self Employment Program for the YMCA of Greater Vancouver, I find my work world is full of assumptions. People come to our program with a business concept that is mostly based on assumptions backed up by research, and then build on it to prepare a business plan. The aim is to validate their assumptions, and yet the outcome is not determined until the plan is implemented. It's a question of confirming as much as we can through research beforehand, then learning as we go and adapting.

With business plans there are many factors to consider: the financial aspects, the marketing research, economic trends, and so on. Working alongside participants, business advisors attempt to take as much of the guesswork out as possible, but there will always be some unknowns.

One of the most significant factors that doesn't show up in a business plan per se is how the business owner is relating to their venture. What assumptions have they made about their own ability to pull it all off? Most entrepreneurs who are able to reach a successful outcome have a strong belief in their ability, the leadership qualities to manage themselves and engage others, and enough confidence and persistence to keep trying until they arrive at a winning formula.

Some come up with a good idea and go through the steps of planning their business but may still not believe they can do it. They have underlying assumptions about themselves that get in the way of having a positive outcome with their launch. As their coach, I always encourage them to keep going, try new angles, and brainstorm solutions. I made a different assumption about what was possible for them because I could see their potential and the way through their obstacles, even if they could not see it themselves.

What if we open up to the possibility that something other than what our mind had predicted based on past experience is going to happen? What if there are other options or solutions just beyond what we currently expect?

Success may rely on the story they tell themselves and continue to repeat. I recall a conversation with one woman who was producing a delicious, nutritious snack product. It was tasty and attractive, and she was in the process of researching distribution channels. In our meetings she would often say, "What if it doesn't work?" I would counter with the question, "What if it *does* work?" Her internal storyline was deeply entrenched, however, and as I recall, despite my encouragement, she did not succeed in the time we were working together.

The problem for many of us is that we believe the stories our minds produce, without challenging them. Or worse, we may not even be consciously aware of a negative storyline. You may have heard about the negativity bias: how our brains tend to remember the bad things that happen to us more than the good or even neutral things. It's a protective mechanism, to keep us safe and out of harm's way. Our brains look for patterns to make things predictable, so it's easy for us to fall into a pattern of projecting negative outcomes on the future and imagining the worst. Then either we don't try, for fear of failure, or we do try, and have our beliefs confirmed when things don't work out. Afterwards, we just accept things at face value and say, "It's just the way it is, and nothing will change."

The people who succeed in business, and in many other aspects of life, are willing to challenge their assumptions about themselves, about other people, and about their situation. They don't accept things as they stand. Instead they are more apt to ask, "What if . . .?"

My journey to coaching

The only constant is change, and while we cannot predict exactly what will change, we know that something will. So what if we open up to the possibility that something other than what our mind had predicted based on past experience is going to happen? What if there are other options or solutions just beyond what we currently expect?

I have experienced this time and time again. While I have often been skeptical and even worried about how events in my life would play out, the most remarkable things have taken place. Things I could not have imagined were just beyond my perception of what was possible.

For example, many years ago, before I became a business coach, I was an administrative assistant for the BCIT Entrepreneurial Skills Training Program. It was a good position and I was capable of all the tasks, but I didn't love doing admin work. Prior to that I'd been doing more creative work in media production, but it wasn't steady work and I needed stable income as a single mom. Working in admin, I thought the program's business advisors had way more interesting work than my own.

I noticed that many participants in the program were overwhelmed by the business planning process, and I would offer an empathetic ear. When there was time, I'd invite them to my office and listen as they "unloaded" their angst. When I could see an opening, I would ask them to take a few minutes to breathe, ground their energy, and let go of their stressful emotions. They would leave feeling much better and able to see next steps more clearly. These were techniques I practised in meditation and healing classes. I had learned how to be grounded, become centred, and keep my energy calm. These practices were great for stress management and included creative visualization.

Hmm, I thought, *working with people like this is way more interesting than scheduling workshops and crunching numbers.* So I started to explore ways to support people in transition and discovered the coaching profession. Interestingly, I saw a small ad for coach training in an alternative newspaper while on summer vacation in Colorado. It said the types of people who could benefit from coaching included entrepreneurs. I e-mailed the organization and asked if they offered training on the West Coast. Yes, they did, and in fact were currently enrolling for training in three weeks' time, in Vancouver, BC!

The coaching program I found was reputable, and it was expensive. I asked if I could use professional development funding through my work to take it, and fortunately the answer was yes. After attending the foundational weekend course, I was impressed that the core principles it was based on aligned well with what I had learned in meditation classes: that we are all creative beings, who have free will to choose for ourselves. Coaching seemed like a practical way to apply these principles.

Training in coaching taught me to ask people questions that supported them in making better choices for themselves. The intuitive awareness I'd gained while learning to be a healer helped me to ask questions that really connected for people. These skills integrated well.

Thinking outside the box

I continued training to be a coach and decided to get my certification. At the time, the assessment process had to be in person, in California. Trainees had their coaching assessed by examiners and wrote an exam. We were also asked to receive coaching from one of the other coaches being assessed.

While I was being coached, I decided to talk about a decision I'd made to move. I wanted to live closer to work and stop wasting time sitting in traffic. Plus, I was spending most of my weekends out of town with a man I was seeing, so my reasons for being close to nature where I was living were not as important. And by then, my daughter had grown up and moved out.

I had been putting off looking for a new place. To me the search for accommodation is a big hassle, and I don't enjoy the upheaval of moving. So while being coached, I decided to talk about how I could approach this using the creative visualization process. I got clear about what I wanted—a place in proximity to work, the right price range, and a move that would be easy; those were some of the criteria. When it came to taking an action step, I said I would use the internal message board at work to post my "want ad." Lo and behold, when I checked the board to see if my posting had appeared, I saw another ad describing a suite for rent, just about a mirror reflection of my request. I called the woman right away, we met that evening, and I had a new place to live. Clearly stating my intent, imagining that it was possible, and taking action allowed me to move past my resistance to what I'd assumed would be difficult.

I waited with trepidation to get the results of my coaching exam, and when they came, I was delighted to be awarded my first certification. To practise my new skills and continue learning, I joined a coaching circle to give and receive coaching. In one session my coach observed that I didn't have much energy or enthusiasm for the things I said I wanted to do. I was being very practical and limiting expectations about what was possible. She challenged me. "What would be exciting for you?"

A few days later, I recounted the conversation while having dinner with the man in my life. He was a spiritual teacher I'd been in relationship with for a few years. He reiterated the question.

"Well, what *would* be exciting for you?" We were sitting in a Greek restaurant that had white plaster walls with blue trim like the photos on the wall of homes on the coast of Greece. The evening sun was shining through the windows, casting kind of a magical spell. "I guess it would be fun to travel," I said, all the while having doubts about how we would be able to afford it. Making assumptions that it was not possible.

A week or so later, my boss came into my office and asked me what I thought about going to Thailand that summer. There were entrepreneurial conferences, part of the APEC meetings there that year, and he and our colleagues in the International Education department thought we should have a presence there. In particular, there was a women's conference that had been identified, and they wanted a woman from our organization to attend. My first thought was: *That will mess up summer vacation plans with my guy.* I quickly thought again. *Wait a minute. That could* be *my summer vacation!*

I said yes to the trip and started making plans to travel to Thailand. I asked if it would be possible to have my significant other travel with me. Yes, he could, I was told. We'd just have to cover his travel costs ourselves. Neither of us had that kind of money at the time. Paying for his travel would mean incurring more debt, which neither of us was prepared to do.

That was also the summer my guy had decided it was time to step down as leader of the spiritual school. He was ready to pass on the role to others in the organization. A celebration was planned to acknowledge his departure—a warm, casual gathering in an exquisite botanical garden. His colleagues and loyal students shared sentiments verbally and some were written in a hand-bound book. At one point in the ceremony, he was handed an elegantly crafted bamboo box. He tucked it away with the book and other gifts he'd received. Later that night when we got to his place, he showed me what was in the box. It was a big roll of cash! His "retirement fund." He now had the funds to accompany me to Thailand. We confirmed our plans to visit for a month, combining my conference attendance and meetings with education reps with a vacation to the southern islands.

Possibilities expand when we're open to change

We had a fabulous time, exploring the local sites—including many temples—on the non-conference days, having Thai massages, and getting gorgeous clothes made. Living the life. We travelled by train to the south islands and chose to stay on Ko Pha-Ngan, where we found a luxurious new beach resort hotel with deeply discounted rooms because there was still construction on site. And we decided to rent a motorcycle to get around the island.

My partner had visited Thailand thirty years earlier and had rented a motorcycle then, but he hadn't ridden since. He was delighted to discover that he loved riding. He felt a sense of freedom he rarely experienced. The joy of those rides planted the seeds for another adventure that involved us both getting motorcycles two years later, but that's a story for another day.

Our trip to Thailand was a magical getaway that we both enjoyed, and I'd been shown, once again, that I could have what I wanted if I suspended my assumptions about what was possible. I could not have predicted being able to make the trip to Thailand when we sat in that Greek restaurant. It was completely outside of my awareness—and yet it happened.

> *Time after time I supported people to question assumptions they held about themselves, what they were capable of, and what they could achieve if they put their mind, body, and spirit towards creating a new reality for themselves as a business owner.*

When I returned to work, I continued in my role as program coordinator. Even though I now had a coaching designation, there were no openings for another business advisor. In fact, my two colleagues who had the position worked well past retirement age, enjoying their stimulating, fulfilling work. I couldn't really see a way to do that work unless I left my position. I think that was also the year I got my five-year service pin from the organization. I shuddered to think about staying there another five years, even though the position meant having security. I couldn't see a way out unless I quit to start my own coaching practice, but that was a risk I was not yet prepared to take.

To my surprise, within a year, I was invited to join another self-employment program as a business advisor. The position was with a smaller organization whose founder was very open-minded and realized how my awareness and intuitive capacity would be well utilized in supporting people in a major transition to become business owners. And I *did* get to start my business,

Living in Vision Enterprises. My new employer required business advisors and facilitators to be self-employed contractors.

The Toward Excellence Self Employment Equity Program targeted diverse groups of people who had faced challenges on their career path due to gender, race, disability, and other barriers to employment. Time after time I supported people to question assumptions they held about themselves, what they were capable of, and what they could achieve if they put their mind, body, and spirit towards creating a new reality for themselves as a business owner. And at the same time, I challenged my own assumptions about my ability to support them.

Most people who become business advisors or business coaches have either obtained an MBA or have direct business ownership experience. I had neither, other than a few years of freelancing in media production. Yet program participants would open up to me because I listened, I didn't judge them, I acknowledged their talents and strengths, and I encouraged them to step beyond their comfort zones. In my business coaching, I learned how to find a leverage point that would move participants past being stuck to gaining traction.

Sometimes getting program participants "unstuck" involved helping them past resistance or an area they felt was a weakness. Many of the creative types I worked with found the task of writing a business plan far too analytical and structured for them to wrap their heads around or put their energy into. In contrast, others were very analytical and found it challenging to think creatively about what was possible. Some literally freaked out about preparing financial forecasts. As I learned more about them and what their mental models and assumptions were, I would validate their strengths, finding a way to show them a new perspective and to trust that they could tackle unfamiliar tasks.

As my own career journey illustrates, checking assumptions, challenging them, and focusing on what you want gets much better results. Assuming something is possible is way more fulfilling than not. In the words of legendary automaker Henry Ford, "Whether you think you can or you can't, you're right." So focus on specific goals and get past the assumptions that hold you back. Thinking about positive outcomes can help you overcome the negativity bias and achieve surprising results.

LYNNE BRISDON

Lynne is a business and leadership coach for those running micro-enterprise start-ups as well as directors, senior managers, and emerging leaders in the education, health care, housing, and environmental sectors. Through Living in Vision Enterprises, she specializes in coaching leaders in new roles with increased responsibility and aspirations to develop high-performing teams. She is known for igniting clients' passion, clarifying their vision, and fanning the flames to energize themselves and attain their higher purpose.

A Master Certified Coach (MCC), Lynne was a past finalist for the Business Coach of the Year Award from the International Coaching Federation's Vancouver chapter, for great business coaching in support of self-employment programs. Her unique approach melds coaching and mindfulness in dynamic, deeply moving ways, leading to practical, applicable results. Her clients thrive by developing self-awareness and their capacity to make better choices and influence others with authenticity and positivity. They improve communication effectiveness by finding congruence between internal sensing and expression.

- 🌐 livinginvision.com
- 🔗 lynnebrisdon
- ✖ @LynneBLIVE
- f LivingInVisionCoach

GREASE, GEARS, AND A GOAL
BY LEAH GILLANDERS

I was very outdoorsy growing up, and that led to an interest in trucks. I wanted to figure out how to fix them when they broke down in the woods. I wanted to be able to do things for myself.

IN A TRADITIONALLY MALE-DOMINATED industry, where grease-stained hands abound and engine revs reverberate, I was determined to defy all odds and establish myself as a force to be reckoned with. I am now a certified BMW technician and respected auto mechanic in the vibrant city of Vancouver, British Columbia. With an unwavering passion for cars since my early days and an unyielding drive to excel, I share my journey as a testament to the power of ambition and determination.

While many children go to sleep dreaming of hoisting the Stanley Cup or becoming a movie star, my mind has always been in a much different place. I would close my eyes at night and picture stepping on the gas pedal, and then envision how everything worked after that. Going through the whole engine was my way of counting sheep to go to sleep.

I was born and raised in North Vancouver, BC, and even when I was young, friends and neighbours knew I was not your typical girl. While my friends were more interested in hanging out at the mall, I rigged up an engine hoist in my backyard underneath the patio. I was going old-school, tinkering on 350 cubic inch small engine blocks in my driveway when I was just thirteen. My insatiable curiosity about vehicles led me to devour car magazines and attend local car shows, further fuelling my love for all things automotive.

My dad is a business owner and my mom stayed home and looked after the family, so as a child and into my teenage years, I mostly taught myself about mechanical things and how they worked. I was very outdoorsy growing up, and that led to an interest in trucks. I wanted to figure out how to fix them when they broke down in the woods. I wanted to be able to do things for myself. I didn't want to have to rely on someone else to fix a mechanical problem. And I still don't!

As I worked through my training, it was tough being one of the only females in the room. . . . Things got even tougher when I decided to fulfill my lifelong dream and open my own shop.

So when I had the opportunity to take an automotive program at Carson Graham Secondary School in 2003, I jumped at it. I dove headfirst into my studies, immersing myself in every aspect of being an auto mechanic. After two semesters, my hard work and determination led to me being offered a scholarship to the Automotive Service Technician and Operations co-op diploma program at the British Columbia Institute of Technology.

No one in my family is involved in the automotive industry. It's just me. I love cars. I'm interested in how they work, and keeping everybody safe on the road is important to me. Years ago, our family vehicle had a blown tire and we didn't know how to change the tire. I didn't like the sense of not knowing, so I was thrilled when I got the BCIT scholarship. I knew right then what I wanted to do after I graduated.

Challenges of entering a non-traditional field

After completing the first year of my studies, I apprenticed for two years at Jim Pattison Toyota in North Vancouver, followed by nine years at Brian Jessel BMW in Burnaby. Determined to prove my mettle, I embarked on a journey to become a certified BMW technician. I spent countless hours perfecting the craft, earning the esteemed title of master tech—an accolade reserved for only the most skilled individuals in the industry. I earned my BMW certificate and became a Red Seal automotive service technician.

I'll admit, as I worked through my training, it was tough being one of the only females in the room. But that was just the beginning. Things got even tougher when I decided to fulfill my lifelong dream and open my own mechanic shop. Reaching that goal meant overcoming many challenges. For one thing, there was very limited space available to lease in North Vancouver, making my search even harder.

When I started looking for a place, landlords who were male wouldn't even give me the time of day, let alone a contract to lease a shop. They wanted to talk to a man and called me derogatory names. No one wanted to lease to a "girl" who was into cars. If I managed to get a landlord on the phone, as soon as they heard what I wanted to do, they'd hang up on me. I had one guy screaming at me, saying he wanted to talk to my boss. And I was like, "I *am* the boss."

I was in tears after talking to some of these people. I almost gave up on my dream of starting my own shop. But as in similar situations in the past—like being picked on when I first started as an apprentice—I just kept going, kept looking until I found the right thing. The right thing turned out to be when I met another woman in the business. She owned a building and was more than happy to lease garage space to me. We hit it off right away. Through hard work and perseverance, I turned my dreams into reality. In 2015 I opened the doors to my new shop, Leah's Automotive, specializing in high-end European cars.

> *The dream went beyond merely fixing cars; I wanted to redefine the automotive service experience. With this goal in mind, I crafted an environment where clients felt at ease, integrating a nail lounge next door to the shop.*

But, as with any entrepreneurial endeavour, my path was not without hurdles. The initial years were rife with challenges, from sourcing the right equipment and hiring skilled technicians to establishing a loyal clientele. The real eye-opener, though, was all the government forms you have to fill out and submit just to open those doors. However, I refused to be deterred by obstacles, and I tackled each challenge with tenacity and unwavering determination (sure, and the odd meltdown).

In 2017 Leah's Automotive earned the Service Excellence Award at the North Vancouver Chamber of Commerce's Business Excellence Awards, being chosen from multiple nominees from all corners of the business world. *My shop!* So many other great businesses were up for this award and I didn't know what to expect. I was so proud of my team and what we had accomplished to receive that award. Hearing the kind words from our clients and what others had to say about my shop was a surreal experience.

An unconventional automotive shop

But it was back to work the next day, so off came the heels and on went the boots, as I had more plans to implement. I love my customers. I truly care about them and their needs, rather than just making the sale. I care about their car, about their family. If they're going on a long road trip, I think about what they would need for that, what they would need to be safe, and what they want to do.

Right from the beginning, my goal was to extend our shop's comfortable atmosphere for clients. People loved hanging out at the shop. Especially during the holiday season, we could have easily knocked down a wall and added another sofa, because people just loved being there. And that's exactly what I wanted when I opened up the shop—to create a place where people aren't scared to bring their car.

The dream went beyond merely fixing cars; I wanted to redefine the automotive service experience. With this goal in mind, I crafted an environment where clients felt at ease, integrating a nail lounge next door to the shop. This unique concept aimed to bridge the gap between automotive repairs and self-care, ensuring that clients could relax and pamper themselves while their vehicles underwent expert care. Leah's Nail Lounge is Leah's Automotive's baby sister and it is the perfect match for female clients—bring in your car to be serviced and have your nails done at the same time. The nail lounge has nine stations for mani-pedis and is mechanic-themed with a feminine flair.

We follow all health standards for sanitation in BC provided by BeautySafe and believe that looking good shouldn't hurt others. I sourced nail polish that is free of dibutyl phthalate, toluene and formaldehyde, which are linked to asthma and allergic reactions, and all lotions applied during the services are organic and animal cruelty free, so you can relax and enjoy them being massaged into your hands and feet. And when you treat yourself to a waxing service at Leah's, my staff never double dip, unless it's salsa on nacho night!

Adding the nail lounge presented its own set of challenges. I had to clean out the storage space of thousands of pounds of used car parts from the previous tenant. I spent hours cleaning the grease and grime from the floors and walls, and then, of course, had to apply for building permits up the wazoo before I was able to build out the space and eventually open. Fortunately, I was getting the hang of filling out forms and knew all the extension numbers to reach the appropriate permit office at the district.

I have never been one to sit still. When I worked with Brian Jessel, he opened up the shop so that I could offer introductory automotive classes for women. These classes were extremely well received, and I wanted to continue this outreach in my shop, so I started the All Girls Garage Club.

I want to help women learn about cars. An automotive shop is an intimidating place for anybody, man or woman, but especially for women. They often feel like they might get taken advantage of or be made to feel dumb because they don't have even the basic knowledge about cars. Their fears might be unfounded, but they still feel that way.

Our classes are small so that when we're learning, especially the hands-on part, women can enjoy their time and have fun. Participants always have some trepidation about not knowing anything, and I really respect them for taking the time to learn. They are showing real commitment. "I'm going to go down to a garage to take off my high heels, put on some boots, and learn about cars." Most women don't want to do that but once they're here, the atmosphere is so much fun. I love it, they love it, and they want more of it.

Despite the immense success Leah's Automotive has achieved, I will always remain grounded. Since I was a kid, I've been enthralled by the inner workings of engines. I love figuring out how things work as well as the thrill of being around cars. My love for cars and the joy I derive from my profession are fulfilling.

Every day, I embrace the opportunity to empower others, especially young women aspiring to break into the automotive industry. Through mentorship programs and speaking engagements, I try to share my story and inspire others to chase their dreams fearlessly, no matter how daunting the odds may seem.

And one last note—everyone always asks what I drive. I love sports cars and love driving them, but what I really love is heading out on the weekend and getting a little muddy. If my vehicle has a mechanical problem out on some remote logging road, I don't have to rely on any help to get up and running. I can fix it with a pry bar and a couple of tools. This knowledge gives me an inner confidence that I want other women to experience as well.

LEAH GILLANDERS

Leah is the owner and operator of Leah's Automotive and Leah's Nail Lounge in North Vancouver, BC. She is a certified BMW technician who fell in love with cars in high school and realized her dream to open her own shop, focusing on European luxury vehicles. She offers customers a different experience by educating them about their car while fixing it, in the hopes of making them feel more comfortable about taking it in to a mechanic. Leah is also one of the very few women in the country to be a Red Seal mechanic—a certification program overseen by the Industry Training Authority that is recognized as the interprovincial standard of excellence in the skilled trades. In 2017 Leah's Automotive received the Service Excellence Award from the North Vancouver Chamber of Commerce.

🌐 autoservicevancouver.ca
📷 @Leahsautomotive
ⓕ Leahsauto

CHANGING THE CONVERSATION
BY HEIDI KILHAM

I have the superpower to carefully choose what I think about and what I believe to be true about myself, others, and events—and thereby to shape my destiny. I am grateful to be part of a community where talking about mental health concerns is welcomed and becoming normalized.

THIS IS A FIRST FOR ME, sharing my story in a written format. While society as a whole is making progress with open discussion, people still don't talk much about the emotional or mental health challenges they face, because of shame and fear of being judged or misunderstood. I'm sharing my journey of processing what happened to me with the hope that if this story resonates with you, you'll know you are not alone.

I've had two life-defining mental health events in my life: a psychotic break when I was twenty-eight years old and a panic attack that happened recently, at the age of fifty-six. I see quite a contrast in context between these events, and I am feeling deep gratitude for the progress I have made. Looking back through the lens of the work I've done with the National Alliance on Mental Illness (NAMI) and in leading study groups on many of Brené Brown's books, I now have language to express these stories in a way that helps me feel more confident, competent, brave, and have compassion for myself.

The crack that let in the light: Workplace abuse

The first event happened when I was newly married, in the early 1990s. I had moved from my family home to a beautiful condo on the water in the Bay Area of California with my new husband, whom I had already known for three and a half years. I had completed architecture school, for a total of seven years of full-time education plus a three-year internship, passed all my licensing exams, and moved about two hours away from the home I had known since I was eleven.

I spent a lot of time alone in those early years, because of the work my husband did and my struggle to find full-time work in architecture. He worked in the video game industry as a programmer, going to work about ten or eleven in the morning and working past 7:00 p.m most days. I kept myself busy by listening to radio shows and learning about living a healthy lifestyle. I changed my diet dramatically; we both lost unnecessary weight. I joined the YMCA and swam three times a week in a masters swimming group. I hadn't made many new relationships yet. Given my husband's work schedule, I realize now that it was a bit too much time alone for me, even though this "loneliness" was normal for me. Remember, there was no googling, Zoom, streaming services, or social media in those days.

After six months of being unemployed, I found full-time work with a small architecture partnership nearby. I thought it would help me feel more confident to meet colleagues and practise in my field. To tell the truth, I barely remember the work I did there, I think mostly upscale home design. I somewhat recall the social engagements my husband and I were involved in with people from his work. This social detachment was a familiar state for me. I was equally detached from my inner life, indifferent to my emotions and what they might mean.

What I did notice was the stark contrast between my hazy recollections of my past and the experiences my husband described. I was uncomfortable with the level of detail he could recall, and I thought he was making it up. I then began to get concerned that there was something wrong with me, since I did not have vivid memories. I mostly remember my childhood through the photographs my mother had put into albums. This concern grew as I continued to compare myself to the one person I was coming to know best, my husband. Also I had few outside relationships to balance the story I was making up about myself.

The traumatizing verbal abuse was perpetrated by one of the executives, so I had a sticky situation where I was praised, appreciated, and validated by one boss and made to feel deeply ashamed, incompetent, and afraid by the other.

When the architecture partnership laid me off, I started at a larger and award-winning firm that was closer to home. Even now, I don't remember details, other than that the partner who oversaw my project was in the kitchenette every day at 5:00 p.m. sharp, making himself a martini. After about six months, he did not give me any more projects, so once I had tidied up the construction material samples and spec library, I think I just walked out because there was no work to do. At this point, I felt like I was floating about aimlessly.

The next job I found was with a single architect who was busy. Unfortunately, she thought my skill set was much broader than it was, and expected me to work independently, without any oversight. I realized that I was looking for a mentor and she was looking for a more experienced architect. We both saw how we had misunderstood each other and parted ways amicably. I was again unemployed and became depressed and forlorn that I wasn't working in my field, not feeling "seen" by anyone professionally.

A few months later, I found work part time in a leadership company as a personal assistant for two different executives. I worked two days for one and two days for the other, with Fridays off. I was intrigued by the job, and I had committed to stay on with the company for a few years, since the work was personally interesting and growth oriented.

Unfortunately, an incident took place just three months into the job that now, in hindsight, I can see was verbal abuse in the workplace. The loud and traumatizing abuse was perpetrated by one of the executives, so I had a sticky situation where I was praised, appreciated, and validated by one boss and made to feel deeply ashamed, incompetent, and afraid by the other. This toxic, bullying work environment led to my first crisis. I believe it was a psychotic break; I was so internalized and inward focused that my mind just cracked.

I woke up the next morning with an auditory hallucination of several radio stations playing at once. My husband was away at a week-long conference. I called the office on our push-button phone and it took me so long to dial, the line kept going dead before I could finish. Once I finally got through, I mumbled that I was not coming in and then hung up. I was alone and afraid.

I could not drive for at least three months as my mind had been flooded and forced open, letting everything in. I honed the skill, while sitting on our couch, of staring out the back windows for hours, lucid dreaming. I don't remember much about what happened during that period and neither does my husband. We were both in survival mode. I did not get any medical attention. Interestingly, at least half of people with mental health challenges (1 in 5 Canadians) do not seek help. I was a part of that number. I did not work again for ten years.

Later I decided to get tested for learning disabilities and found that I have an auditory processing disorder, or APD. I process verbal instruction at a much slower pace than most people. This would have been helpful to know much earlier.

I became disenchanted with the workplace setting and shifted my focus to creating a better life with my husband and to starting a family. Without family support, we decided that the most nurturing work I could do was to develop myself along with our growing daughters. By then, we had created a life and relationship that could withstand this dramatic change. I am extremely grateful for the opportunity to have supported his professional growth and success these many years and that we could live well without my income. We talk often about the "design" level of what he does as well as business trends and corporate leadership.

Since then, we have moved countries and medical systems. We now reside in North Vancouver, BC. We have two talented and beautiful daughters in their early twenties and my husband has forty-five-plus years' experience in electronic video game creation. I managed to meet another architect close to home a year and a half after we moved, when the girls were settled in school. I worked with him part time for ten years as an assistant designer. I am deeply grateful for his accommodations and mentorship. He recognized the areas in which I was strong and he graciously restructured his workflow to give me the tasks I did well. This was a very validating and healing experience for me. He was the mentor I had sought so many years before. I felt seen, heard, and appreciated. I will never forget his generosity in spirit and in deed.

Learning and growing in community

Coming to Canada after 9/11 was the beginning of a whole new journey regarding community. Our daughters were enrolled in a school that placed a large value on community, and there were many opportunities to engage through school activities. The Vancouver Waldorf School also attracted families from all over the world, so we had a diverse group of peers. Many sought out the school specifically because of the pedagogy.

This community has supported me in making some long-term relationships besides that with my husband, to whom I had disproportionately compared myself. Neither of us grew up in a community per se that we felt a part of, so this experience was not only healing for me but also healing for my husband, as we integrated ourselves into a new culture, a new livelihood, a new home in every sense of the word.

Now that we are firmly rooted in North Vancouver and our daughters are finding their way and settling nearby, I am developing a new level of community through my volunteer work. Our youngest daughter was hospitalized and diagnosed with anxiety disorder and bipolar I disorder when she was almost seventeen years old. This was a defining moment in our family, when we became painfully aware of something that was right in front of us. We desperately needed to adjust our expectations, hopes, and fears regarding these mental health conditions as well as face the associated guilt, shame, and self-judgment.

> *My self-confidence and competence received a big boost being surrounded by such healthy, positive, young, and extremely knowledgeable personal trainers. However, even with all this strong, solid, encouraging support, I experienced a panic attack.*

Fortunately, in 2017, my husband and I found an education program called NAMI Family-to-Family, a free eight-week course for any family member or friend with a loved one who lives with a serious mental illness (SMI). We are both deeply grateful for our re-education through this course, helping us to adopt a blame-free attitude about serious mental illness in society. Our whole family was fragile and raw during our daughter's recovery, which honestly is an ongoing challenge. We practised what we learned in the course, and we were deeply moved by how many others in our community were taking this course. There were fifteen in our class and three other classes about the same size at the time. We had no idea how common serious mental illness is in the population. We found strength in knowing that we were not alone.

By early 2019, I had trained to become a leader to facilitate the Family-to-Family course for other family members. I had come to learn that my *lived experience* is valuable and was precisely what qualified me to become a leader. Now, five years later, I am a NAMI leader trainer, co-training leaders to facilitate this same course in BC. Our daughter also gives presentations about her experience living with now three SMI diagnoses to high-school students and faculty.

While supporting our daughter through the ups and downs of her recovery, I was able to retrain as a professional leadership coach. I decided not to continue in design when my mentor and friend chose to retire. I also followed in the footsteps of my father and began weight training in earnest in June 2021. At fifty-six, I'm probably stronger than I have been my whole life. In 2022 I had the opportunity to go back to work full time as an office manager for the personal training studio where I started my training. My confidence and competence received a big boost being surrounded by such healthy, positive, young, and extremely knowledgeable personal trainers. However, even with all this strong, solid, encouraging support, I experienced a panic attack.

Normalization and reaching out

I have come to learn just how common panic disorders and attacks are. At least three out of four people I have talked to have either had a panic attack, had multiple panic attacks, or know someone who has. Statistics Canada states, "In 2013, an estimated 3 million Canadians (11.6%) aged 18 years or older reported that they had a mood and/or anxiety disorder." They further report: "The one-year prevalence rate [of social phobia, one of the most common anxiety disorders] in Canada is 6.7%; in the U.S., it is about 7%." And according to the National Institute of Mental Health, anxiety disorders in the United States affect an estimated 31.9% of adolescents between 13 and 18 years old.

The book *Unwinding Anxiety*, by Judson Brewer, is a particularly helpful resource due to its straightforward approach in describing anxiety as primarily a habit loop that can be skilfully redirected. I'm grateful to have been trained about SMIs and to have taken the Mental Health First Aid course, offered by the Mental Health Commission of Canada, which helped me to identify this extremely uncomfortable experience as a panic attack. I recognized this theme repeating itself from my first event so many years ago—feeling confused and light-headed by the paradox of what was occurring in my life in the weeks and months leading up to it.

On the one hand, I was a successful manager and facilitator fully engaged in an upbeat, accountable, and growth-oriented culture. On the other hand, I was accused of being personally diminishing, dismissive, and cruel to an outside colleague. My mind could not comprehend this divide, which led to a tightening in my chest, shallow breathing, and feeling utterly distracted by these sensations. This all occurred while I was driving, and I was fully aware that it was not safe to continue. My mind was racing from one thing to another, feverishly trying to solve an unsolvable puzzle.

Fortunately, I have been a part of a movement to destigmatize or normalize the feelings of depression, anxiety, and other mental concerns. Recognizing I was experiencing a panic attack, I had the presence of mind to call someone I know and love who has experienced this in his life. He picked me up metaphorically and literally and helped me understand and recognize that a panic attack is a real medical condition. He talked me through exercises to calm myself and allow the attack to pass all while holding my hand. I was hyperventilating, so he coached me how to breathe more slowly. I spent the next three days mindfully breathing in quickly and breathing out as if I were blowing through a straw. This helped reduce my symptoms dramatically by shifting me from a fight-flight-freeze response to a more regulated state.

Because of my many past conversations with this wonderful young man that came to my rescue, I felt little fear of dying. I felt obsessed with what was going to happen at work, with my extracurricular activities, and by how many people I was letting down. I used the following week and a half to calm my mind, take cold baths, sleep when I needed, have facial stretch therapy (FST), and engage in nurturing conversations with people I love. All this helped me to process my experience.

I'm beginning to recognize how the stories I make up about myself and my "performance," and especially obsessive thinking in comparing myself to others, *only* lead to a state of mental overwhelm (crisis). I know now that there's nothing wrong with me. I have the superpower to carefully choose what I think about and what I believe to be true about myself, others, and events—and thereby to shape my destiny. I am grateful to be part of a community where talking about mental health concerns is welcomed and becoming normalized. My daughter and I are passionate about "anti-discriminating" mental health concerns. We hope that by telling our stories and supporting others to seek education, we can encourage others to connect to the burgeoning peer support and lived-experience mental health movement.

I thank you for reading my story. If any of my lived experiences resonate with you or someone you know and love, please know that you and they are not alone. Many people and resources exist to support a healthy and sustainable recovery and to help you live your best life. I am one of them.

HEIDI KILHAM

An enthusiastic, thought-provoking, and sincere facilitator with the background of a California architect meets dreamer-thinker, Heidi has expertly designed her life to maximize peace of mind as an ICF-certified co-active coach and mother. Heidi is deeply curious about development of all types, from building environments to leadership, from trauma recovery to weight training. She is an Associate Certified Coach (ACC) as well as a Certified Professional Co-Active Coach (CPCC).

Heidi also serves in the capacity of leader trainer with the National Alliance on Mental Illness, co-leading further development of the Family-to-Family education program and others in BC. She lives in North Vancouver with her husband of thirty years and two adult daughters.

When she is not strength training, you can find her in nearby Lynn Canyon leading hikes and exploring new trails.

Heidi works as an office manager for Innovative Fitness, North Vancouver, a premier personal training studio.

✉ HGKcoaching@gmail.com
in heidi-kilham-acc-cpcc-46857944

STRENGTH IN RESILIENCE
BY LISA HUPPÉE

Becoming a franchise owner was the opportunity I needed to show that I was truly capable of achieving my dreams. Sometimes opportunities find us when we are not expecting them. It is up to us to decide to take a chance on ourselves.

IT TAKES MILLIONS OF YEARS of intense pressure for carbon to transform into an authentic natural diamond. The result is precious. In life, we all face struggles, setbacks, and moments of intense pressure. Just like a diamond, I have experienced forces that could have worn me down but been resilient despite what I went through. In the face of these challenges, I have become an authentic person with sparkle and strength.

Regardless of who you are or what path you choose, difficulties await. Growing up in a small Alberta town, I was under immense pressure to be the perfect student and figure skater. My mother was focused on results and driven to ensure that achieving success in school and in figure skating was my top priority. This focus on success led me to be unaware of my needs and well-being.

Figure skating taught me that life is not just about doing something to the best of your ability, for there will always be external factors that can affect the score and the results of your hard work. It taught me there is always room for interpretation. As a people pleaser who sought approval and love, I always tried to do things perfectly. Yet these attempts often went unnoticed and were under-appreciated. My mother was narcissistic and the abuse I experienced as a child was overwhelming. Not until later was I able to understand the toll this had taken on my mental health and sense of self-worth.

Around the age of twenty, I realized I was never going to be able to please my mother and make her proud. I decided to stand up for myself and express my feelings surrounding perfectionism and the abuse I had endured. My relationship with my mother ended abruptly when I asserted myself and moved out of the family home. I was told I could "never come back" and that I had made my bed and had to lie in it. This moment changed my life forever. I realized my mother was never going to change and that I needed to start a new life on my own. (My father and I were not close. He told me when I was nineteen that he was disappointed I was not a boy and that he didn't think I was his child. That is why he never wanted a relationship.)

A part of me knew that life had to be better than this. In my schoolwork and competitive figure skating, I had been so focused on results and the opinions of others, on being perfect. For years, having goals and achieving them was the *only* thing that mattered. I came to realize that while this is a good thing, it is not the only thing. When I was young, whenever I experienced pleasure in something, smiled, or laughed, my mom would say, "Life isn't fun!" This narrative framed my perspective for many years. I believed that happiness and joy did not exist in the realms of career or life purpose.

My outlook was clouded by my mother's own trauma. I was living in the shadow of her negativity. It was stifling, and not until I decided to stand up for myself and to choose my happiness did I feel free to be myself. I moved out while I was attending university, and I began to develop a deeper understanding of myself and my desires.

Perseverance through years of turmoil

Although I felt that I was choosing myself for the first time in my life, I was still on a career path that had been chosen for me by my mother. I was in school to become a teacher. In truth, I loved kids and I deeply wanted to make a difference in my work. I decided to continue on this path but to reframe this choice as my own. Even though I still felt insecure and unworthy, I knew that if I worked hard and kept my goals in mind, I could achieve success.

It wasn't easy, being in the world on my own. I struggled financially to afford university courses. I worked hard to pay my bills, and I lived with roommates to save on my expenses. In the late 1980s, it was quite unusual for a young woman to have two male roommates. I was ashamed of my living situation and afraid of being judged. As in the past, I thought I would only be seen for my faults and flaws, but I kept going.

The longer I was away from my family and the damaging narratives I had grown up with, the more I started to sparkle. I ended up meeting someone who saw my value. He saw me as pretty, intelligent, talented, and sweet. I truly felt that I had found my special someone. He encouraged me to follow my passions and to finish my degree. At last I felt respected and loved for who I was.

We married and had two children. My life was finally coming together. But there were many challenges yet to come. After I was married for about five years, I discovered that my husband had a secret life. Drinking, drugs, and gambling were more important to him than his family. I tried to help him overcome his addictions and make better choices. I tried to forgive him and see past his faults. Eventually, he suffered a heart attack, but instead of changing his ways, he started using harder drugs and sank deeper into his depression.

By then my kids were teens and we had all had enough of the lies, chaos, and betrayal. I never thought my marriage would be such an embarrassment. I was not a drinker and I had never used drugs. I had tried so hard to make our relationship work. And now I saw that my efforts were all for nothing. This betrayal was beyond devastating. I had poured everything into this marriage and the life we had. In the end, my husband chose destruction. Because he would not leave, I had to sell the house to get rid of him and be able to move on.

> *Resilience is defined as the capacity to withstand and recover quickly from difficulties. It is a skill, like any other, that you practise and get better at.*

My life felt totally out of control like it never had before. Being on my own was frightening. The shame was on my ex, but I felt people judged me and thought less of me for his actions. On top of that, I felt guilt for what I'd put my kids through. I was mentally exhausted and scared financially, but I was also determined. I had to get two part-time jobs on top of my teaching job to make ends meet, tutoring in the evenings and painting apartments on weekends.

This period of my life felt like a whirlwind. I tried desperately to focus on what I could control to rebuild and start over yet again. I focused on my relationships with my kids and my friends. I eventually started dating again. I also joined a Divorce Care group at my local church and I took a course on boundaries. At the time, this was the best thing I could have done for myself. It completely changed my life. I finally understood that my husband's poor choices were not my fault.

I began to understand how to take control of my boundaries and how to move into new relationships without baggage. I started standing up for myself when I felt used or disrespected. I regained confidence in myself. My life by age forty had been fraught with financial, emotional, and family challenges. I didn't want to be a bitter old woman who resented people and situations, stuck living in the past, unable to move on. With conscious effort, I opted to shake off the negative stuff and look for the good in life and in myself each day.

Resilience is defined as the capacity to withstand and recover quickly from difficulties. It is a skill, like any other, that you practice and get better at. Having looked at my part in my marriage and taken responsibility for enabling my husband, I was finally able to grow and move on. This allowed me to be healthy in my self-esteem and in my boundaries, and enabled me to openly love again.

Overcoming obstacles, gaining confidence

At this point I was in a teaching role at a local elementary school. My life was finally starting to feel secure and stable. I had come so far from the fearful and self-conscious version of myself that I used to be. Unfortunately, there were more challenges ahead.

At this school, I was being micromanaged and harassed by an administrator. Because of what was going on, I started to hate teaching, something I had always loved and worked hard to do well. This administrator had repeatedly stopped me from being able to transfer to a different position and different workplace. I felt trapped and unhappy yet again. This time, my stress sent me in a new direction. Instead of trying to repair what was broken, I looked for new opportunities. I chose to be assertive, proactive, and pivot away from the abuse. To increase my work options, I took design courses online on my own time. But each time I drove into the school's parking lot, my entire body was telling me I didn't want to be there.

One day, as I was talking to a fellow teacher during recess, I felt an immense pressure, as if someone were sitting on my chest. I listened to my gut feelings and went to the hospital to get checked out. There, I learned that the cause of this pain was stress. I talked to my doctor and explained what I had been dealing with at work. He told me to take a stress leave and to seek counselling. Due to my unhealthy work environment, I was in fight-or-flight mode. I had gone from my divorce right into another stress-inducing situation.

I listened, taking time away from the career path I had worked towards my entire life. That summer, I chose a new path altogether. I started working as a designer, project manager, and owner at Rational Kitchens, which imported modern high-end cabinetry from Germany, and took a risk doing something entirely different. I now had a whole new roster of responsibilities: talking to builders on site, connecting with designers, and helping customers find solutions.

I was still that shy, insecure little girl from a small town. I pushed myself to learn, to go out every day, and to step beyond my comfort zone. At first my days were full of scary conversations with strangers. I felt self-conscious and unworthy all over again. Soon I started to gain confidence in my abilities. I also came to recognize the way I was talking to myself. My inner narrative was that of the limiting beliefs my mother had imparted to me. I began to realize that my success was up to me, and with the right mindset, I could escape the old narratives that kept me stuck.

Through self-reflection, I discovered that I wanted to use my talents and experience to build something meaningful. I wanted to feel connected to a greater sense of purpose and to be able to really help people through my work.

My time spent working with designers was challenging. I felt judged by them, for they made me feel small and lacking important knowledge. In the end, my employment with that business did not work out the way I had hoped. My take-away was that sometimes people want to see you fail, and sometimes they will try to sabotage you. But instead of choosing bitterness, I chose to break the thought pattern my mother had instilled in me.

I realized I was not the failure I perceived myself to be. I took an opportunity to try something new, learn from my experiences, and develop my resilience.

Taking risks to realize a dream

By the time I left that job, I had remarried. I faced some challenges with having a blended family, but given the hurdles I had encountered earlier in my life, I felt I could get through anything. Focusing on love and talking about our challenges as a family allowed me to thrive despite obstacles. At the same time, feeling pressured by my new husband to have a full-time job and learn sales skills, I decided to take a job in sales. However, in this new role, I did not feel that I was using my talents in any way. I felt uninspired and disconnected from my work. I felt stuck, yet again. Rather than standing still, I elected to work on myself, investigating my deepest inner self and my motivations. I wanted to feel more connected to my work and my sense of purpose.

Through self-reflection, I discovered that I wanted to use my talents and experience to build something meaningful. I wanted to feel connected to a greater sense of purpose and to be able to really help people through my work. I began to brainstorm. I had plenty of ideas, but every time I ended up coming back to senior care. I had always loved seniors and helping seniors. I had administrative experience, caregiving experience, and a strong relationship with my maternal grandparents. I was drawn to home care based on my experience tutoring and teaching kids, which I had done for years. I wanted to open my own business to use my skills on a larger scale.

As I was gaining clarity on my goals, I faced some serious health issues. I had my gallbladder removed and went through a period of recovery. Although this setback pushed me further off my chosen path, it also made me feel even more motivated to accomplish something meaningful.

I researched home care / senior care companies and franchises for about a year. I felt called to work that would allow me to support others and encourage them to make a difference in their communities. With my husband's input, in August 2019 I decided to buy a Just Like Family Home Care franchise in the Fraser Vallery. The move seemed like a huge risk and financial outlay. Seemingly overnight, I had become the owner of a company! However, this company had no staff, no clients, and a loan to repay. I was on the precipice of yet another major life change. I had no idea what I was doing, but was determined to figure it out.

Yet, because I was on unfamiliar ground, I was also returning to some of my fearful beliefs. My self-limiting narrative was creeping back in. Nobody in the Fraser Valley had even heard of Just Like Family Home Care. I was losing confidence before I even got going. I felt simultaneously overwhelmed and excited. Once again, my negative self-talk was trying its best to keep me down, but in the spirit of resilience, I carried on.

Being goal-driven, I began to work my butt off. I put all of my energy into building this business from the ground up. It was just me in the beginning; I was playing every role this company had to offer. I sank myself fully into the business, working non-stop, without days off. I pushed myself as hard as I could. And then in March 2020, COVID-19 put everything on pause. The pandemic was yet another obstacle in what felt like a never-ending succession of hurdles. This new setback was scary because of its many unknowns. But since I had put everything I had into this business, I was not about to give up. Marketing in person wasn't possible and hospitals didn't want visitors. Despite the many challenges, I kept trying and implementing new marketing strategies. Who knew when the pandemic would end?

In May 2020, an opportunity to purchase the Richmond/ Delta franchise location caught my attention. I didn't know what was going to happen, but I knew I had to trust my intuition. My husband and I had worked to build things together. We got another loan and decided to take the risk of adding another franchise to our growing franchise "family." The main challenge in that location was hiring and onboarding staff. At times we lost clients due to being unable to get the staff we desperately needed.

In the face of adversity, resilience helps us overcome misfortune and frustration. It helps us survive, recover, and even thrive. Fast-forward to 2022, when we purchased the Tri-Cities location in April and acquired the West Vancouver location in May, by paying cash. We paid off our initial investments by persevering and choosing to take a small salary. Recently, we purchased our fifth and sixth locations, on Vancouver Island.

Looking back, I have come a long way from that shy, self-conscious little girl who didn't like to make waves. I never anticipated I would be this successful in a career. I have undertaken every aspect of running the locations: hiring, scheduling, payroll, billing, caregiving, managing, training, designing training modules and HR and office protocols—you name it. Becoming a franchise owner was the opportunity I needed to show that I was truly capable of achieving my dreams. Sometimes opportunities find us when we are not expecting them. It is up to us to decide to take a chance on ourselves.

My biggest lesson has been learning to trust myself fully and make intuitive decisions in my business. All the difficulties I have overcome throughout my life have made me the person I am today, and although my path has been far from easy, I am incredibly grateful that I persevered. Having resilience is the key to getting through the unexpected, even when hurdles seem insurmountable. The greatest compliment I have ever received was that someone looked up to me for being resilient and not letting obstacles stop me.

Perseverance and resilience have been integral to my success. The intense pressures I have faced throughout my life gave me the sparkle and confidence in myself that I always needed. I learned that it is possible to receive great rewards through hard work and that I can make a real difference in the world. Now I am living my purpose. Just like a diamond, my strength is my power, and I choose to shine my light for others to see.

LISA HUPPÉE

Lisa is the owner of six Just Like Family Home Care locations throughout Metro Vancouver and on Vancouver Island, BC, providing quality in-home care for people of all ages, abilities, and backgrounds. Her journey to becoming a franchise operator was far from straightforward, but she believes that with perseverance, we can accomplish great things.

In 2022 the Fraser Valley location of Just Like Family was voted best in Home Health Care by CommunityVotes Abbotsford. Such local awards serve as a reminder that finding a deeper connection to one's work can make a world of difference. When not working, Lisa has time for painting, meditating, and expanding her spiritual interests. She now has the freedom to travel when she wants to, a supportive and loving husband of nearly ten years, and is living the life she has always dreamed of, tucked away in the mountains with the people and pups she loves.

- 🌐 westvancouver.justlikefamily.ca
- 🌐 richmonddeltabc.justlikefamily.ca
- 🌐 fraservalleybc.justlikefamily.ca
- 🌐 nanaimobc.justlikefamily.ca
- 🌐 westshorebc.justlikefamily.ca
- 🌐 tricitiesbc.justlikefamily.ca
- in lisahuppee

TRUST IS THE NEW LOVE
BY RINO MURATA

I had absolutely no idea what I was going to do, other than knowing things had to change. I didn't know what to change, so I decided to drop everything we were doing. No more school. No more activities. No more tutoring. Full stop.

TRUST IS ONE OF THE MOST OVERLOOKED emotions, with the potential to either destroy a person's life or help it to flourish. We think we know what trust is and what we need to do, but trust is also one of the scariest emotions to fully embrace.

We can guess why we have trust issues in our relationships. And by relationships, I include those with intimate partners, friends, colleagues, ourselves, society, and even—especially—with our kids. I often wonder how different my life would have been if my parents had had full trust in me. It's likely that I would not have been burned out and severely depressed for two years when I was nineteen. It's very likely I would not have married my first husband, and very likely I would have trusted my own inner voice and not have neglected my physical and mental state until it was almost too late.

I believe trust, or the lack thereof, is what changes the course of our lives. With trust, we are able to believe in ourselves, know that we are capable and have all the resources we need to achieve our goals. We can have faith in the unknown. Lack of trust, in contrast, will make us feel "not good enough" and afraid to face challenges. Lack of trust will hinder us from making the changes we need to make in life. Without trust, we might not try at all.

Trust is the new love. Most of us are really good people. We are caring; we love deeply; we are kind and compassionate. We love to be of service to others and are good stewards of our community. Our businesses and missions are built from our sincere desire to make the world a better place. In my opinion, there is an abundance of love in the world. I think we can all agree that love is at the foundation of it all, but not necessarily always the factor to actualize one's purpose and meaning in life. Then there must be a very important element we tend to overlook. There must be a component that bridges love to the life we want to live. I think trust is that bridge. My parenting journey—with its early frustrations, eye-opening epiphany, and abrupt change of course—illustrates the profound power of trust as an expression of love.

The story of my three sons

I became a mom to my first son when I was 26, had my second son at age 29, and the third one at 31. Every time I held them in my arms for the first time, I told them, "You are perfect." The love I felt for them was out of this world, and it is hard to believe how much stronger it has become over the years.

It bewildered me when I was pouring my life and heart into my "perfect" children that the world didn't seem to see them that way. Take my eldest, Joey. His speech development was not "age appropriate." He wasn't learning how to read like "other children." By the time Joey was seven, he'd attended two kindergartens and three schools where all the teachers said, "We don't know what's wrong with Joey." On the last day of school when Joey was five, the principal even said, "This child doesn't have time." In Hong Kong's extremely competitive school system, Joey had already missed out on getting into one of the good international schools.

The psychoeducational assessment Joey had at age six showed he had almost every learning disability. Dyslexia and language processing disorder did not come as a surprise, and he was diagnosed with autism spectrum disorder later on, at age fourteen. I did everything I could to help Joey because I loved him: taking him to speech and occupational therapies, tutors, abacus classes, swimming lessons, and horseback riding. We moved back and forth between Tokyo and Hong Kong five times in search of the best possible school, one that would give Joey the support he needed.

I cried a lot during these years. It hurt me to no end to see how my child was being perceived and why Joey wasn't "good enough" to the world (schools *are* the world, if this is all you know). I had meetings with school administrators, headmasters, and teachers almost every week, to discuss Joey's study plans; half of the time I spent pleading for them to see Joey's potential and talents and not give up on him.

Joey ended up being expelled from an international school in Tokyo when he was in Grade 2, on the day of the Christmas concert. According to the headmaster and the elementary-school principal, Joey wasn't showing the progress the school wanted to see. As I looked at a crèche set up at the entrance to the school, including the stable where Jesus was born, I wondered if there really was a God. I couldn't fathom how a child could be kicked out of school because of his learning speed. I was in a mess and bawled when the second-graders sang during their performance. Joey didn't know that he would not be returning to this school after winter break, and there he was, performing with gusto like young children do. They were all adorable. Joey was only seven, and the world had already rejected him.

It felt like the world had closed its door on him. I thought Joey would no longer be successful in life. I worried he might never be happy. He was bullied in every single school he went to. I thought: *He'll be ostracized by society now he's been kicked out of school. He is on the track to being stamped as a failure. There is no amount of love that can protect him . . .*

At this time, I still struggled to accept that there were other ways to raise and educate a child, so not going to school wasn't an option yet. I registered Joey at our neighbourhood Japanese public school, which he attended for the remainder of Grade 2 and most of Grade 3. The school wasn't ideal, given Joey's language processing disorder, since I had chosen English to be the main language we used at home. My two younger sons also started to attend a nearby Japanese kindergarten. I prayed that things would be better for Joey.

To be honest, meetings with teachers continued. At about this time, Joey began to lose sleep. By age nine he had insomnia and couldn't fall asleep. When he finally did, he would wake up every two hours. Joey also started to have stomachaches and headaches in the morning, so he was absent from school more frequently. Also, there were signs that something was wrong not only with Joey but also with Andy and Toby.

Andy, now five, had developed obsessive-compulsive disorder (OCD) seemingly overnight when he was three; he wouldn't wear anything except a Superman costume day and night. It had to have a cape. Also, he was not able to step on any sort of line or cracks, whether tiles or bricks on the pavement. There are a lot of these cracks when it's an issue. To top it all off, he developed tics where he would constantly be shaking his head, as if to say no. Andy was officially diagnosed with OCD, along with anxiety, several years later, when he was ten.

Meanwhile Toby, my youngest, was a happy chap every morning, excited to go to kindergarten, but only until we arrived. Once there, he threw up every single day, and I would either bring him back home with me or the teachers would try to comfort him and tell me, "He'll be fine! Go!"

One evening, I scolded Joey for being slow in doing his homework. Joey went to his room, so I went in to persuade him to come sit at the table and finish his work. Joey was crying and yelled at me, "I HATE YOU!!" I tried to hold him, but he wouldn't let me.

The following day, while I was in my car alone and waiting for the traffic light to turn, a question popped into my head that changed the course of my life and very possibly those of my sons. As I wondered what I was doing wrong for Joey to hate me, the question hit me: *Would I have any regrets if Joey were to die tomorrow?*

The answer was a no-brainer. All I would have would be regrets. Why didn't I raise him just as himself? I would ask myself. Why didn't I let him do what he enjoyed? Why did I make him study until late at night so he would get good grades? For what? Why didn't I protect him? What was I trying to do? Besides future questions, I had one in the present moment. What had happened from that day Joey was born and me thinking *You are perfect*, to now my son hating his mom and not letting me hold him? Slowly, the answer was revealed.

What had happened was *my* perception of Joey had become skewed. Joey never changed. Joey was being himself. Everyone else was trying to make him into something he wasn't, and I was completely unconscious of the fact that I was at the forefront of it all. Andy and Toby were already showing me signs that school

> We all know the importance of allowing children to follow their curiosity, but for many parents, this is easier said than done. It definitely was for me.

was not working for them. I thank the universe for bringing what is important in life to my attention. Was going to school like everyone else more important, or was my kids' well-being and the relationship I have with them, the person I show up as for them, more important?

Turning to trust as my guide

I had completely lost trust in myself to see Joey for who he truly was. I didn't trust that I knew my child better than anyone in the world. I was way too afraid to trust that I was capable of paving a different path for my children. But I'd be damned if I was going to ignore that question that came to me while waiting for the traffic light to turn.

I had absolutely no idea what I was going to do, other than knowing things had to change. I didn't know what to change, so I decided to drop everything we were doing. No more school. No more activities. No more tutoring. Full stop. The board of education in Tokyo didn't know what to do with me when I told them I was no longer sending my kids to school. I told them they should come to check on me unannounced to make sure I was not abusing or neglecting my kids. They never did, though.

This was the moment I turned to trust to be my guide. Everything would turn out beautifully, beyond my wildest dreams, if I let trust lead the way. Everything I did next stemmed from connecting with my gut feelings for life to blossom the way it was intended for each one of us. I was not able to imagine the outcome for my boys. I basically had to let go of anything I thought my children could become. Their destination was not mine to determine. Trust was about giving my all without expecting an outcome. I didn't know I was tapping into trust, but I was.

Home-schooling is not legalized in Japan, but I did it anyways. No one I knew was home-schooling, so all I had was my intuition telling me what to do next, what to read next, and which movie, documentary, or YouTube video to watch next. We tried all sorts of different home-schooling methods and failed plenty. I soon noticed that despite them all being mine, each of my kids learned differently. Their interests were different. Their skills and talents were different. I felt this was important information to take notice of and not brush off as just common sense.

Since that moment at the traffic light, one huge question that lingered over my head was "What keeps a person alive in their darkest hours?" Initially, I thought it was love. But that answer did not add up. I loved my children fiercely, and yet here we were. There was something else. The sequence of questions, one leading to another, that arrived over a few years went something like this:

- What one thing would keep you going when you had no one to turn to, feeling all alone in the world?
- How do I raise humans that are authentic and accept themselves for who they are and also know they are good enough?
- What is the one thing we are all born with that we lose along the way, a loss that makes us feel disconnected from our true selves?
- How do we cultivate and keep the fire going inside a person with passion, interest, and curiosity, not judging what interest is better than another?
- What does this all mean?

All these questions had answers that came full circle in the end. Those answers were either trust, passion, or staying authentic, and they led me to unschooling. It was imperative for my kids to know they were enough and worthy just the way they are. Authenticity is most easily achieved when we allow our children to follow their passion, curiosity, and interests without judgment. Passion and curiosity are qualities that every single human is born with and that children have an abundance of. We all know the importance of allowing children to follow their curiosity, but for many parents, this is easier said than done. It definitely was for me.

> *Being given the opportunity to trust my boys gave them the power to be focused in life and diligent in working towards their dreams, in ways beyond anything I could have ever imagined or taught them.*

For instance, I used to set strict screen time and limits to technology for Joey, Andy, and Toby. When I relaxed those rules, I found it hard not to judge what video games my boys wanted to play and also not judge myself for allowing them unlimited screen time. My new way went against so many parenting beliefs, but I had to trust the principle of trust. Trust cannot be conditional.

The magic of radical trust

So here it is. The final answer to all these questions was trust. I learned through unschooling that I could trust that my children were born and equipped perfectly with what will guide them to live the life they were meant to live and be the person they are. Passion, interest, and talents are not something to be found when you're eighteen, thinking of what you want to do with your life.

Everyone is inherently born with these traits. It is up to us as caregivers to let our children follow, discover, and nurture their passions so they never lose the spark and have to search for it again. My job as a parent was to create the space and support for my kids even if I didn't know what any of their interests were going to lead to. I had to trust the process. Trust that my kids have everything they need.

(You might be curious to know what happened when my boys had unlimited screen time for years. The result looks different for each of them. Video games are not a novelty for them but still important to Joey and Toby. Andy, too, when it involves playing online with friends. But they are not so obsessed with video games that they lose sight of their goals and aspirations in life. And game play has never interfered with them being responsible for their school work, once they went back to the school system.)

If you made it this far into this chapter, you may be wondering, "Where's the dad?" I did have a husband, and my children do have a father. He is a very successful businessman who is following his dreams and passion. He is very good at what he does, and I would say he did make his dreams come true. But he was not much part of the journey my children and I took. He and I parted ways because, during all the questioning, I was finally forced to face what authenticity meant to me. It was crucial that my boys would see me walk the talk. There was nothing more excruciatingly difficult—and nothing more important—than trusting my gut, accepting who I am, and pursuing my personal happiness.

Being given the opportunity to trust my boys gave them the power to be focused in life and diligent in working towards their dreams, in ways beyond anything I could have ever imagined or taught them. And trusting myself allowed me to break free from expectations and end a marriage, which opened the door to meet my second husband. In our relationship, we both feel fully content and finally feel good in our own skin.

Joey is now eighteen and in film school, following his passion. He received a 100 percent mark from all three teachers for his capstone project in high school. Andy is diligently working towards his dream to become an NHL player, despite starting to chase that dream very late, at the age of thirteen. He knows how far behind he is compared to his peers that have been skating since they were three, but he believes in the power of discipline and dedication. His progress is remarkable. Toby benefited the most from unschooling, being the youngest one, and has always been following his passions for go-kart racing, cars, and numbers.

I'm going to let you in on my secret. I used my kids as guinea pigs to test out my theory of radical trust. I had no idea how parenting based on trust was going to turn out. All I knew was that trust worked in theory, and it made sense. It was up to me whether I believed in it and let trust work its magic. I would like to close this chapter by saying with full confidence: trust works.

RINO MURATA

Rino is a relationship coach who helps clients get their romantic relationships right by getting a clear understanding of themselves through a holistic body-mind-soul approach and emotional intelligence. Rino believes love and relationships are worth pursuing. She discovered through parenting her three sons that love itself cannot build a strong and healthy relationship, but being able to have mutual trust, honesty, and respect is what makes relationships meaningful to everyone involved.

A certified Integral Life Coach and certified Trauma-Informed coach, Rino holds a bachelor's degree in sociology from Sophia University in Tokyo. When she is not working or furthering her training to be a better coach, Rino enjoys cooking for her blended family with five kids or zoning out in front of the TV, not remembering until the very last moment the show she is watching for the third time.

rinomurata.com

rino@rinomurata.com

NECESSITY, AN AMAZING MOTIVATOR
BY PAULA SKAPER

Adopting a digital operating model for your business is at once a lot less complicated than you fear it will be and a whole lot more challenging than you ever imagined. But in the end, it's worth it.

"WHAT SHOULD I DO?" It was February 2020. The woman on the other end of the phone was watching the emerging news about COVID-19 and she was worried. "Naomi," a mentor for women business owners, had a business that depended on women getting together in person for intensive three-day retreats, multiple times each year. The public health lockdowns that were starting to ripple through the world economy meant she could book no more retreats. Cancelling the primary revenue driver for the company would mean the end of her business.

When Naomi called late that Friday afternoon, I was a lot more optimistic than she was. I've enjoyed a front-row seat to society's digital evolution since I started my career in the early nineties. I've helped hundreds of companies in industries ranging from internet start-ups to bricks-and-mortar retail stores embrace digital transformation. It's been a lot of fun, but it hasn't always been smooth sailing.

What I've learned from those experiences is that adopting a digital operating model for your business is at once a lot less complicated than you fear it will be and a whole lot more challenging than you ever imagined. But in the end, it's worth it. Every single time.

Naomi, like thousands of other business leaders worldwide, had to confront the reality that the way she had done business for the past thirty-five years would become impossible within the next few days. Since she had absolutely no digital component to her program and no way to engage the women in her community outside of live events, it seemed—to her at least—that her business might not survive the pandemic. In the same moment that she was feeling panic, I was feeling excitement at how a change could improve her business. And I knew without a doubt that her business would not only survive, it would thrive. For that to come about would require completely transforming the way the retreats were run, with only twelve weeks to make this change happen. Fortunately, we had one critically important factor on our side.

When the status quo no longer works

There is something reassuring about having things work the same way as they always have. We're hard-wired to protect "the way we've always done it." Don't believe me? How many times have you heard someone shoot down an idea with some version of the following? "We tried almost exactly that a few years ago and it didn't work. It won't work now either." And with that, any notion of change is soundly dismissed. Except . . .

When the status quo isn't an option, the biggest barrier to change is instantly erased. With no comfort zone to default back to, the question of what to do changes. I could hear panicked acceptance of unavoidable change in my client's voice. I recognized it because I've been there myself, more than once.

My first remote work experience arrived in 1997. I was seven months pregnant with my first child, but my vital statistics were not good. I had pregnancy-induced hypertension—a potentially life-threatening condition with only one cure, childbirth. My only job for the next few months was to survive long enough and stay healthy enough to give birth. My doctor ordered complete bed rest until the baby was born.

> When I opened my own business nearly twenty-five years ago, the first thing I did was make sure every person on my team was set up to work from home if and when they needed to.

This was something of a problem, for my partner and I needed my income to stay afloat. Early maternity leave was not an option. I had to reinvent the way I showed up at my job so I could follow my doctor's orders *and* keep my income flowing. Just a few months earlier, my employer had provided me with a modem at home. In the middle of launching one of Canada's first-ever online publications, I needed to better understand the commercial internet from a user's perspective. Somehow, I convinced my employer that I could work from my home office until the baby was born.

For the next fourteen weeks, I worked from a reclining chair beside a makeshift desk next to the crib in our nursery, feet propped up on a stool as per doctor's orders. I ran my department and trained my maternity leave replacement with no connection other than a phone, an e-mail address, and a 14400 baud modem that connected me to the internet. It was an imperfect solution, but it worked.

Two years later, in 1999, while working as a senior account manager at an internet firm, I arrived at work one morning to find the entire office under two feet of water. Once again, necessity demanded action. Within 24 hours, everyone was able to work remotely from home. For the next month, the entire company operated virtually. No deadlines were missed and our clients really didn't care, as long as the work got done.

Both times, an unavoidable change in the status quo without warning opened my eyes (and those of the people around me) to new ways of working that had previously been inconceivable. So, when I opened my own business nearly twenty-five years ago, the first thing I did was make sure every person on my team was set up to work from home if and when they needed to.

That flexibility in when and where to work proved very attractive to moms with young families. They were more than happy to trade a slightly smaller income (at my small business) for the significantly lowered costs that came with not needing before- or after-school care. Plus, they had the convenience of not counting sick days or taking vacation time when their little ones were home with a fever. I didn't realize it at the time, but we were pioneering the world of hybrid work. So, by the time covid hit, I had been managing hybrid teams for more than two decades. I was less afraid of remote work than some other businesspeople, because I had already experienced it.

I brought that experience into my conversation with Naomi, walking her through how online meeting tools could be used to get the women together, even in the face of public health restrictions. This would simply require a few adjustments to how her events were structured. Of course, figuring out what technology we would need was the easy part. It always is. The real challenge is never the technology.

People trump technology

One of the most painful lessons I have learned is that it doesn't matter how smart the plan is or how sexy the technology is, if the people on the team don't support it, the plan will fail. Passive resistance is a powerful force. Almost as powerful as unrecognized roadblocks.

One of my first experiences as a digital transformation consultant involved working with the US headquarters of a large international bank to launch their first foray into online banking. It had never been done before. Every word, every line of code was scrutinized. Getting approval on a single paragraph of copy took over a month.

Our team was frustrated. We were getting nowhere and we couldn't understand why. Communication felt like we were speaking different languages, and we questioned whether the client's team was actively working against us. Eventually, I flew to Buffalo with a few of my colleagues to try to move things forward. On the first day, I met with the senior VP of marketing for the bank. She took me back to her office to figure out how to solve the problems she was experiencing with testing the website. What I discovered stunned me—we had completely overlooked a critical piece of the puzzle.

She explained to me that no matter what she tried, she couldn't figure out how to get the website to open on her computer. She looked up at me, frustration evident on her face. "I feel so stupid. It sounds so easy, but I don't know what I'm doing wrong."

This lovely, brilliant woman had been following my instructions to the letter. But my instructions were incomplete. In order for them to work, she needed a computer that could access the internet. She required a computer equipped with a colour monitor, running the newer Windows operating system, and it needed to have web browser software installed.

Spoiler alert: the VP's cubicle featured a desktop IBM running DOS, with a monochrome monitor. Security protocols in the bank meant that she had no direct connection to the internet. There was absolutely no way to open a web page. I had assumed that as the senior VP in a large international bank, she would have the latest computer equipment. I assumed wrong.

She gave me an amazing gift in that moment. She taught me that any technology implementation will succeed only if you approach it with a people-centred strategy. Ever since, I have made sure I understand the mundane challenges that face the people I am working with. So, when it came to helping Naomi pivot her business for a post-covid world, I knew that the people running the mentorship program were going to need the most attention.

It took mere minutes to put the technical solution in place. The technology needed is quite simple and inexpensive. The people pivot would be harder. Volunteers leading her retreats ranged in age from 30 to 70, running small, local businesses. Most barely used a computer in their day-to-day work. Several had never even heard of a Zoom call, let alone been on one.

Naomi and I let all seventeen women know that the next retreat would be held online and that we would spend the next twelve weeks making sure every one of them was comfortable running a meeting in this new format. Job one was to introduce Zoom and make sure everyone was comfortable working in this new format.

I created a set of instructions for how to set up a free Zoom account, download and install the software, and log in for the first time. I sent it to each of the women and asked them to help me make sure the instructions were clear, because this same document was going out to all the women in the program. By turning their own challenges into a way to help others, we encouraged each woman to reveal any struggles right away.

For the next few months, I held weekly practice meetings with Naomi's leadership team on Zoom, gradually introducing and practising new skills each week. We also made sure everyone was comfortable with the slice of their personal life that would become their on-camera background. We helped figure out camera positions and rehearsed where to look when addressing the online participants. Anyone who wanted to was invited to book a one-on-one call with me to practise Zoom basics and troubleshoot technical issues that came up.

We decided that the women who were more comfortable with the technology would act as meeting hosts. They would be responsible for opening "rooms" on time and providing tech support to participants during a call. This strategy ensured that only a handful of women needed to really learn the technical ins and outs of Zoom call management. The women delivering session content would partner with the meeting host but wouldn't need to worry about operating Zoom and could focus on delivering a great experience—exactly as they had at the in-person retreats. We also adjusted the schedule for the day to accommodate the reality of participants being at home, surrounded by family life.

> *Every one of us needs windows of calm between periods of rapid change. Without them, people tend to become either actively resistant or passively apathetic, because they are worn out from simply trying to keep up.*

By the time the event came round in June, we were ready. The three-day online program went off perfectly, and the women who participated were thrilled with the experience. For her part, Naomi realized that this new format now empowered her to reach a wider market. The online model was more profitable and made it easier for women to participate by eliminating the need for travel. The retreats remain virtual to this day.

Incremental steps with breathing room in between

Any time I've been through several changes in a relatively short period of time, my psyche needs time to adapt to this new way of being. Without these "stability breaks," I can get emotionally and mentally exhausted, which usually shows up as foggy thinking, silly mistakes, or lowered productivity. This is called *change fatigue* and it's very real.

Every one of us needs windows of calm between periods of rapid change. Without them, people tend to become either actively resistant or passively apathetic, because they are worn out from simply trying to keep up. By the time change fatigue takes hold in your team, there's not much you can do except try to keep things on an even keel while everyone regains their balance. So it's imperative to be proactive and educate people about the condition before it happens.

We've all just lived through a perfect example of change fatigue in action—the COVID-19 pandemic. Overnight, many of us were forced to work from home, to hold meetings on Zoom, to shop for groceries online, to teach our children Grade 9 science *and* math, and figure out how to protect our family from COVID-19 while renegotiating sharing space with them every day—and doing it all at the same time. Just as you began to get the hang of it all, many of those changes were reversed. Then reinstated. Then reversed again. And again.

Think about your own reaction to the pandemic. Most of us will admit to at least some level of "not being at our best" by the end of 2022. I heard from clients that they felt foggier, were having more trouble making big decisions, weren't sleeping well, or just didn't feel motivated or excited by their work.

Most of the time, we don't have anything as dramatic as a global pandemic driving the changes we are implementing. When getting where you want to go involves a massive change, try to make small, incremental changes over time so that each step builds on the previous one. Allowing some breathing space between each successive change, to give everyone enough time to get comfortable and familiar with the change that's taken place, might make it feel like you're going more slowly, but in reality, you'll get to the finish line much faster this way.

I stumbled across this strategy very early in my career while running the production department for a publishing company. Magazine layout was still a slow, manual process, prone to errors. Even though advances in design and printing technology were making faster, easier options accessible, our company was entrenched in the way things had always been done.

My team and I developed a plan to gradually bring the company into the digital world, testing one small change at a time. It took us a little over six months to convert our entire production process to the new method of publishing. Over the half-year transition, no one outside our department knew what was happening. They *did* feel like we'd become a little more relaxed when they missed a deadline, but they didn't know why.

When I finally announced to the whole company that we had just shipped our first ever digital-to-print issue of the publication, my colleagues were excited but unsure what it really meant or why it mattered. It mattered because we could now

- provide an ad materials extension that allowed sales reps to close two extra pages in ad revenue
- accommodate a late editorial change without incurring extra production costs
- reduce annual pre-press cost for each of the five

publications we produced by roughly $40,000—a total annual savings of $200,000

- ship each publication early for the first time in company history, with fewer errors than any previous issue

The change worked as well as it did because we took slow, incremental steps. We validated the viability of each tiny change, before rolling it out to all publications. We redesigned processes and put checks and balances in place to avoid potential disasters. And we did all of it without materially changing anything about the work that other departments needed to do.

Unknown to me then, we had instinctively hit on one of the golden rules of instigating change inside a resistant organization. If you can implement changes incrementally, without disrupting the operations of other teams, it's worth taking the extra time to make it happen.

Here's the most important lesson I've learned. Technology changes everything and nothing, all at the same time. There isn't a single area of business today that hasn't been impacted somehow by technology. And the pace of change continues to increase. Human beings, in contrast to technology, have remained fairly constant. People today tend to think and act much the same way they did at the start of my career.

Technology's true value has never been its ability to replace human beings. Its value is in its ability to free up people to reach their full potential. Digital adoption changes the work people do, but you will always need good people to operate and manage that technology. Necessity is an amazing motivator, and people make transformative change happen.

PAULA SKAPER

A leadership and digital transformation expert with a proven track record of driving organizational success in today's rapidly evolving business landscape, Paula has spent more than two decades helping companies navigate the complexities of digital transformation and harness its potential for growth. She is the founder of 33Dolphins Growth Strategy, a management consulting firm that helps businesses to embrace and leverage digital advances that drive revenue growth, while improving operational efficiency and enhancing customer experiences.

Recognizing that successful digital adoption is about more than technology, Paula emphasizes the human element, ensuring individuals and teams are equipped with the skills and mindset needed to thrive in the digital era. Her unique approach uses comprehensive strategies that align technology, people, and processes to achieve sustainable and innovative change. Paula has a profound impact on the companies she advises, empowering teams to embrace digital tools and unleash their full potential.

🌐 33dolphins.com

in company/33dolphins

EXPLORING, DISCOVERING, CREATING
BY CHRISTINE B. HENRY

I had never been able to confine myself to a single career path, and yet it had never occurred to me to combine all my passions into one harmonious whole.

I WAS INCREDIBLY FORTUNATE to have enjoyed a fulfilling career in visual merchandising and design for three decades. I affectionately referred to my work of dressing mannequins, creating in-store room sets, and designing window displays for major retail store chains across Canada as "playing Barbie" and "playing house." However, my journey took an unexpected turn when I was laid off in 2008, at fifty-five years of age, due to what my employer called budget cuts. I was devastated and unsure of what to do next.

Finding similar jobs in the evolving era of retail, where stores focused on optimizing every square inch of floor space, proved to be challenging. Initially, I was filled with anger, and to cope with the stress, I found myself cleaning, rearranging my home, painting walls, and decluttering. But these diversions provided only temporary relief. My mind was spinning with ideas on how I could generate income to help pay the bills.

Preparing a resumé was difficult, since I had not needed one for a long time. And the work world had changed drastically. Display jobs were becoming obsolete, and I didn't have a lot of experience with balancing books or working on computers.

I diligently searched for work, applying for numerous jobs daily. Part-time, full-time, anything. But when no opportunities presented themselves, I began to feel inadequate. My whole career to date had been focused on creativity, not technology.

Desperate, I called a friend, who arranged for me to be interviewed for a job as receptionist/billing clerk in a physiotherapy office, which I then took on. Wow, did I find out quickly how I despised computer work. Each patient had several insurance providers, which all needed to be billed separately, with certain portions billed to each insurer.

Disheartened, yet determined to conquer these new skills, I stayed late evenings to catch up and be prepared for the next day's onslaught of patients and billing. Pushing myself too hard to be perfect, I began to experience a few panic attacks on the job. My heart pounding, tears welling in my eyes, hands shaking uncontrollably, I would run to the washroom. Talking to myself, I tried to convince myself I could do this; I just needed to keep trying.

I persevered for a few more days, until one late evening, I was exhausted and ended up pulling all the wrong day's charts from the file cabinets. I felt as if I were going to pass out. I sat down in the office chair, elbows on the desk, with my heavy head being held up in my cupped hands. Crying, I vowed, *This is it. I'm done. It's not worth it to experience this much unhealthy stress.* I couldn't even see the names on the charts through the tears in my eyes.

After a minute or so, pulling my shoulders back, I got up to refile the incorrect charts and quickly pull the correct ones. Nodding my head with conviction, I stated, "There. Done." As far as I was concerned, those were the last charts I would ever pull. Smiling, I locked up the office, turning the key slowly for the last time. I experienced such relief when that door closed and I looked forward to discovering what door would open next. Quitting was going to be hard to explain to others, but for me I had absolutely no regrets.

My husband took my departure from the office job surprisingly well. He knew me better than myself sometimes. The physiotherapists were not as understanding, but they were glad I decided to leave sooner rather than later. The search for employment was on yet again. I needed a job with variety, creativity, and the freedom to use my time efficiently, but in my own way.

Exploring diverse creative options

Unemployed once again, I considered the possibility of working from home or starting my own small business for a second time. I had learned a lot from operating my special events decorating business on the BC mainland, one of my many on-the-side business ventures before moving to the Island. Creatively it was rewarding to transform a bare hall into a magical, romantic, welcoming venue. That work was like my older retail display days but with more freedom. I hadn't really considered starting it up again on Vancouver Island. I was happy with the new retail display job I had landed when we'd moved to the Island for my husband's new position. Until, of course, the layoffs began. Maybe now was the time to explore options such as decorating or maybe staging homes. I was grasping at straws.

My supportive husband encouraged me to take some time to refocus and discover new interests. He said not to rush into anything. I eagerly embraced the opportunity and began taking watercolour painting lessons and writing classes, and I joined a photography group called the F8s, named for a middle camera aperture. Although I had no clear vision of how these pursuits could translate into a money-making venture, I found the process of learning and interacting with fellow creatives to be great fun and inspiring.

Watercolour painting was delightful but not a good fit for me. Just like the sketch class I attempted, where drawing a stick figure was the extent of my talents. Writing was an interesting ongoing activity, but photography seemed to interest me the most. As a group the F8s took nature walks and visited raptor centres to practise our photography. We explored derelict buildings and made field trips to fascinating locations all around Vancouver Island.

It was an intriguing proposition to be paid for doing something I loved. Could this be another new adventure or a pivot in focus from selling photo prints on canvas to doing event photography?

Our photo group decided to participate in an art exhibition, for which each of us needed to print one or two of our favourite shots onto canvas. The show was a huge success. Soon I found myself printing more of my work, creating a collection large enough that I could present a solo show at a popular coffee shop. I sold most of my prints, with one going all the way to Uganda to grace the walls of a newly built children's school. Excited by the results of the show, I joined a collective art gallery and took part in many festivals, markets, and more coffee shop shows. Being interviewed on three separate occasions by local newspapers was exciting. One of the articles featured a photo on canvas piece I had done, which resulted in a reader contacting me to buy the picture.

Rejuvenated with hope, I decided to delve deeper into the world of photo art. I invested in a brand new laptop, a powerful photo editing program, and a five-colour printer. I joined a phenomenal online course called Photoshop Artistry with Sebastian Michaels. I devoted every waking hour to learning new techniques, capturing new photo assets, printing my images, and selling cards and canvases. Christine Henry Arts was born, with associated business license, business cards, website, truck decal, and all. Now it was time to start networking.

Discovering a passion for photography

To broaden my horizons and expand my network, I began attending networking lunches, chamber of commerce events, and various women's groups. I relished observing everything around me, particularly at these types of gatherings, where people-watching intrigued me. I started bringing my camera along to candidly capture special moments: the expressions on people's faces, their eye contact and body language, and the warmth conveyed through handshakes, hugs, and smiles. It was all mesmerizing.

To me, it was crucial to capture the full event. Through my candids, I strived to weave a story with a beginning, a middle, and an end. I sought to unveil the backstage intricacies, the inner workings that often go unnoticed: the set-up process, the flurry of food preparation, and the tireless dedication of the unsung heroes, the volunteers. My work was not only about recording the main event; it was about the whole event. I wanted to create more than just a collection of images that anyone could capture with their smartphone.

Inspired by these events, I would eagerly return home to review and edit the photos I had taken. I enjoyed the process of cropping and enhancing shots of the attractive, intelligent, and energetic businesspeople I had the pleasure of meeting. One day a group leader approached me, expressing interest in using some of my photos for their marketing purposes. Caught off guard, I stumbled but ultimately agreed to her request, emphasizing that I had invested considerable effort into editing each photo to ensure that everyone looked their best.

She offered to compensate me for my work, and also expressed an interest in hiring me as their group's event photographer on a regular basis. I was upfront with her about my lack of technical camera skills and proper equipment. I also cautioned her that posed shots didn't interest me in the least, except when they involved capturing an old barn or a rusted relic of a truck in the midst of an overgrown field. I reiterated that I was a candid shot photographer with a storytelling element to my work. We shook hands, exchanged information, and set the date for the next event, where I would present her with a fair invoice.

It was an intriguing proposition to be paid for doing something I loved. Could this be another new adventure or a pivot in focus from selling photo prints on canvas to doing event photography?

The more events I attended, the more doors opened, leading to an array of exciting opportunities. Soon I found myself immersed in candid photo shoots for political candidates as they canvassed at special events. The hustle and bustle of charity fashion shows was invigorating. I guided young children on photo shoots in nature, opening their eyes to a new way of perceiving the world through the lens of their smartphones. A super fun event was when I embarked on a three-day photo shoot in a cold, rainy, and lush forest, capturing high-school boys taking an extracurricular course experiencing the arborist's way of life. Even construction companies wanting candid "working" shots for their marketing materials began to seek me out.

As my work in photography progressed, I made the conscious decision to set aside the busy markets and solo shows. The physical demands of setting up heavy display grids and awkward tents, along with transporting my canvases, proved to be extremely arduous. Carrying only a camera and one spare lens was much more manageable.

Crafting an abundantly creative life

As I focused on candid event photography, I continued to explore other avenues of photography art. While editing event shots, occasionally I'd get sidetracked, playing with interesting Photoshop tools and tricks I had learned in the course I was taking. What fun to totally transform an average shot into a work of art!

The Photoshop Artistry course instructor encouraged creativity of all kinds. One of the lessons was to merge writing with images. The possibilities were mind-boggling. As I searched through my parents' photos to use for the project, interesting details of my ancestors were revealed.

The idea of heritage pictures merged with nostalgic stories made my senses tingle with excitement. I lacked the ability to draw or paint like my talented artistic parents, but digital art and writing gave me the tools to create endlessly.

> *I learned to make moccasins, ribbon skirts, hooded blanket coats (capotes), pemmican, jams, and bannock. I stumbled through beginner language classes in Michif and jigging dance classes too.*

While enjoying all my successes, I began to explore further my Métis culture and heritage—something that had been kept secret for many years. When I was growing up in Manitoba, my infuriated father would only ever tell my brother and me that we were French Canadian, period. No other details about our roots were ever shared. Later in life he explained that if people knew we were Métis, he might not have been able to attend the art school he and Mom went to. Nor would we have been able to purchase the wartime home we lived in.

Continued curiosity fuelled my desire to learn more about my background. By joining a Métis local community group, I met four inspiring women. Each is dedicated to teaching and sharing their cultural knowledge. I learned to make moccasins, ribbon skirts, hooded blanket coats (capotes), pemmican, jams, and bannock. I stumbled through beginner language classes in Michif and jigging dance classes too. The art of beading was relaxing—and a fun little extra money-maker as well, when I sold pins in various designs that I beaded by hand.

As I was learning these cultural skills and making new connections, the COVID-19 pandemic disrupted the world. Through that time the five of us—Jo-Ina, Marlee, Carmen, Mariana, and me—continued, when possible, to safely meet outdoors, masked and socially distanced. These meet-ups of the Maamashkaach Métis Mamas (*maamashkaach* means "awesome" in Michif) resulted in the creation of a photo history and videos of how-to Zoom sessions and Facebook posts, with each of us sharing our own skills and showcasing the expertise of our mentor, Jo-Ina. Once again, even during the coronavirus pandemic, my photography had a purpose—visual history in the making.

Once things slowly opened again, people were starved for connection and camaraderie. Family meant more; memories meant more. I was busier than ever as a photographer, capturing important moments in so many people's lives.

But I felt the urge to do something crazy and fun for my sixty-eighth birthday. Something just for me. Going on a women-only guided e-bike trip from Victoria to Tofino, BC, was just the ticket. Our group had a blast, and the photos I took would be part of many art projects to come. Invigorated when I returned home, I decided to continue my adventures. A solo road trip to visit my grandchildren, whom I hadn't seen for ages, seemed to be a great idea. It would coincide with meeting up with the Maamashkaach Métis Mamas at a huge Métis festival called Back to Batoche Days, in Saskatchewan. I drove from Victoria to Winnipeg, stopping in each province to connect with family and to explore, building up my photo image files with shots of nature, landscapes, derelict structures, and cultural event images.

Eight weeks later, I returned home with thousands of photos to go through. I had enjoyed seeing the grandkids so much that I decided to volunteer at a Métis daycare and helped occasionally at elementary schools with "the girls." Kids have that innate ability to make everything so much fun. Hugs, energy, and huge smiles abound. More daycares were about to open on Vancouver Island. They needed to attract more caregivers, so they needed marketing photos of the tykes enjoying their days at the culturally built facility. Leaders, Elders, and schools needed a visual record of their programs to submit with their grant requests. Here I was again doing what I loved, resulting in more photography contracts.

Then out of the blue, one regular medical checkup turned into a year filled with doctors' appointments, stress of the unknown, and then surgery. Everything was a whirlwind of confusion, for I felt fine, as though nothing was wrong, and considered myself quite healthy. But the diagnosis was a slap on my wrists for not keeping up with regular checkups for over five years. Now halfway through my sixty-ninth year, happily cancer free and recovered from surgery, I pick and choose which and how many photo jobs to take on.

I found time to work with all the images I had collected on my trip, turning them into not just edited photos but into photo art that was published in international photo artistry magazines such as *Living the Photo Artistic Life* and *Awake Photography*. I also wrote short stories that were published in numerous books, including *The Community Book Project: Celebrating 365 Days of Gratitude* and *Woman of Worth: Empower with the Power of Collaboration*.

This was the pinnacle for me—an existence filled with a sense of purpose and an abundance of creative expression. I had never been able to confine myself to a single career path, and yet it had never occurred to me to combine all my passions into one harmonious whole. Having multiple creative pursuits gave me the freedom to choose my focus at any given moment, whether it was diving into the depths of digital artistry, writing short stories, digitally capturing the true essence of special events, or seizing the joy of cultural connection and Métis heritage.

From my very first networking event where connections were forged to the rewarding moment when I received my first paid opportunity, my journey has been an adventure of exploration, discovery, and boundless creation. It is a balanced life I cherish—a life that will continue to bring me joy well into my senior years. Exploring, discovering, creating.

CHRISTINE B. HENRY

Born in Winnipeg, Manitoba, Christine was happily raised in a very creative family.

She is the mother to three talented sons and the proud grandmother of six creative grandchildren who constantly inspire her to explore, discover, and create.

Christine is a freelance photographer, capturing Métis events, nature, rusty old relics, landscapes, and simple everyday objects that spark fond memories of carefree days of exploration on the Prairies and now the beauty of Canada's West Coast.

She is a digital photo artist, a writer, and published author of non-fiction short stories who candidly captures the essence of special events and life's cherished moments.

Christine is presently exploring her Métis heritage while working on her own book and hopes to encourage women of all ages to cherish connection with groups that explore a variety of adventures, to discover the joys of their own inner creative selves.

- 🌐 ChristineHenryArts.com
- 🔗 Christine-henry-982a6b27
- 🅕 ChristineHenryArts2

THE JOY OF ENOUGH
BY MARILYN R. WILSON

The idea was startling: I personally am enough just as I am, with all my quirks. I am not lacking any key ingredients and do not need to reshape myself into someone who fits in a box. I am enough.

ENOUGH. I have come to love this powerful word. Growing up in a small town in the '50s, it felt normal to me to live in a constant state of lack. My family and most of the people I knew were of average or below-average means, so I fit in with my social group. Didn't most kids have one pair of shoes and get one present at Christmas? Didn't most families have holidays where they camped in a trailer their father built from scratch, or visited relatives' homes where the kids all slept on old-fashioned air mattresses?

However, underneath the surface, hidden deep inside me, a seed was planted. This kernel would grow into an unwanted weed called scarcity. It was nourished by the image I was presented with daily of what my future life would most assuredly be. My journey would be like that of my parents, one of never having quite enough. Lack of money would always be an issue. Financial success would never be in the cards.

As the weed called scarcity grew and spread, this invasive plant sprouted a new belief that proved even more damaging—it was selfish to crave a healthy bank account and covet fine things. To focus on or strive for financial success would somehow tarnish my soul. Getting ahead wasn't viewed as a sin exactly, but money was seen as something a truly good person wouldn't think about or reach for. To be a good person meant sacrificing my own wants and desires, to always put others first and put myself last. Any person worthy of admiration and love spent their lives giving fully, a belief served, of course, with a side of "lack" and seasoned with a dash of struggle. Only selfish people focused on accumulating wealth and possessions.

Since this was the only vision I was given as a child, the possibility of a different future never occurred to me. Leaving home at a fairly young age, I was soon immersed in low-paying jobs. They fit the expectations I had grown up with. No one had ignited a fire in me or shown me how to fan the flames of hope for a better future. There was no passion calling me and I had no dream to reach for.

I was never taught to create a budget. Why would I bother? Extra money would never be part of the equation. Life was only about having enough cash to cover rent, food, clothing, gas, and car insurance. I never imagined myself travelling the world or owning a beautiful home. Having a healthy bank account was a pipe dream. Then I fell hard for an amazing man.

Fortunately, my life partner, who also grew up in scarcity, had parents who believed working hard and budgeting wisely were stepping stones to a better future. I was encouraged by his confidence, but struggled to silence all the negative tapes running in the background—lessons from my childhood that still haunted me. We had very little at first, which didn't help. I found myself often frightened by dark thoughts of our finances falling apart and worried we would never have enough. Credit cards were my downfall during times when I struggled to make ends meet, especially when it came to spending on my kids.

All three of our children were targeted by bullies at school. The side effect was they became socially isolated. Classmates avoided spending time with them, fearful they would suffer the same fate. To soften the impact this had on them, I kept them engaged with tons of outside activities. Unfortunately, the cost to keep them busy was way more than what we had available. A few times I had to have a hard talk with my husband about the bills I had run up. I was lucky to have a partner who loved me as I was and, instead of getting angry, lovingly helped me to see a different way.

I gave up the joint credit card with the high limit and applied for one in my own name with a very low credit limit. This low-limit card enabled me to take care of small purchases but helped me avoid running up a large balance. A side benefit was the chance to build credit in my own name, something I lost when I moved to Canada after getting married. My partner also took over our finances. I was grateful to let go of the responsibility, yet I wasn't left out of the conversation. We spoke often about budgets and goals; I was included in a way that helped me learn.

To help save money, we spent our vacations camping and visiting family, the same as we did while I was growing up. We took the kids to visit relatives on the farm in South Dakota one year and drove around the clock, having them sleep in the minivan so we could avoid paying for hotels. One year when things were really tight, I came up with something I called "Vacation in Vancouver," where we did all the things tourists did when they visited our city.

Along the way, shame and frustration would still raise their ugly heads. I remember looking around one day at all the couples we knew who were far ahead of us financially. They had married at a younger age, both worked full time for a few years, and bought their first house before starting a family. Their homes were nicer than ours and renovated regularly; their holidays were higher end, presents more deluxe, and the whole family skied in the winter. I experienced overwhelming feelings of jealousy and wished for our lives to be less challenging. I yearned for prosperity.

> *Enough. Enough. Enough. Each time the word arose, it was like a pebble being dropped in my pond, creating ripples of change.*

After two decades of hard work and sacrifice, our house was finally paid off. Being rid of our mortgage was so freeing, but it wasn't an easy goal to achieve. We chose not to renovate or buy expensive furnishings. My husband did most of the house repairs himself. As the houses in our neighbourhood were being torn down to make way for larger homes, we ignored a lot of repairs as a waste of money. By the time we sold our home, it was in bad shape. Because of this, I was embarrassed to invite friends over, but found our choices were validated when we sold the place. The first thing the buyer did was bring in a bulldozer.

With the house paid off and the kids off on their own, our savings began to swell for the first time. What a novel experience. Suddenly the chequebook no longer needed to be balanced in fear every day. I didn't have to be as careful buying groceries, and we could eat out once in a while. Maybe we weren't yet living the lifestyle of our peers, but we could finally breathe.

Over the next few years, I came to fall in love with the word "enough." The word first tapped me on the shoulder while I was reading a book by fellow author Danielle Rondeau titled *I Am Enough*. The idea it offered was startling: I personally am enough just as I am, with all my quirks. I am not lacking any key ingredients and do not need to reshape myself into someone who fits in a box. I am enough.

My journey to self-acceptance continued as the universe kept finding new ways to whisper this truth. Enough. Enough. Enough. Each time the word arose, it was like a pebble being dropped in my pond, creating ripples of change. And every time this happened, I found myself reacting physically—there were goosebumps.

Images offering a different kind of future began to rise. These images felt foreign, as I had never imagined a life without endless worry. At the same time I found them strangely comforting. At first I didn't give these images much thought. They appeared. I reacted. I moved on. I am grateful that the universe did not give up on me. The nudges kept coming.

When I look back, it was as if I had been sleepwalking through life. Then one day everything shifted. I don't recall the exact moment I finally opened my eyes. I simply remember it felt like waking from a dream and seeing the world as it is. In that moment I chose to pause, sink in deep, and focus on why the concept of "enough" kept appearing in my life.

I came to realize that lack did not exist the way I thought it did. Being in a permanent state of scarcity wasn't a blessed place to be, or one that would bring me more love. My husband and I were no longer struggling financially. My children had become amazing adults, doing a great job of handling their own lives. We had great friends, a pantry full of food, a comfortable home, and the ability to travel. I was surrounded by abundance.

A line from Brené Brown's book *Daring Greatly* resonates with how I have come to feel about the idea of living a life of contentment. "The opposite of 'never enough' isn't abundance or 'more than you could ever imagine.' The opposite of scarcity is enough. . . ." Take a breath and read that again. Let it sink in deep. Inhale and repeat the word "enough" as you exhale.

The concept we usually hold out as a goal is abundance. The best definition I have read for this word is "to have more than you need." Experiencing abundance means your cup is not only full, but overflowing. You can use that abundance to help others who are struggling. However, it's not a great idea to connect your happiness to always being in this state. Prosperity comes and goes.

When considering the word "enough," I find myself most drawn to this definition: "sufficient, in a quantity or degree that answers a purpose or satisfies a need or desire." Having enough means my needs and desires are met. Having enough walks hand in hand with contentment. The day I realized the joy of enough, my world shifted. I began to let go of my never-ending worries about our finances suddenly falling apart.

Embracing the belief that you have enough doesn't mean being careless. My husband and I are still thoughtful in how we spend. While we aren't flying first class, we travel in a way that both works for our finances and gives us joy. This has helped us let go of feelings of guilt or worry over what we spend. Money is a blessing. Trying to hold onto it too tightly and hoard it possessively simply means living in a constant state of fear. Our focus is on finding the right balance in our spending.

> *Discovering the joy of enough has allowed me to dive deep into what I want for my future. While I am always thoughtful in my spending, . . . I have let go of the need to desperately accumulate wealth.*

My partner's guidance was very important in changing the message I received while growing up. One of my high-school girlfriends never married, but she found a different kind of support. She connected with a financial advisor that was a good match. Once she retired, they worked out a budget that included not only her living expenses, but also money for travel and for any keepsakes she buys on her jaunts. If anything happens to my partner, I will definitely consider working with an advisor to keep on track financially.

When I look at the next generation coming up, I see them struggling with the idea of enough in a different way. Many are now raised with high expectations paired with the adage "You can achieve anything you put your mind to." Success is goal driven. They are encouraged to be doctors, lawyers, CEOs, and successful entrepreneurs, to travel first class, enjoy luxurious holidays, and live in expensive homes. The focus is totally on the image of what society labels as financially successful.

While it's great to set the bar high and aim for the skies, the pressure to succeed this attitude places on our kids can be overwhelming. Focusing only on status and income can create feelings of failure if the life they end up living doesn't fulfill the dreams and visions they were fed while growing up. One of the choices we made with our kids was to expose them to all kinds of careers without judgment. Their life—their choice; no pressure.

At this point, I would like to address the idea of "enough" from a more practical standpoint. Learning to embrace the idea you have all you need—no matter how small that might be—speaks to those who have their basic needs met. Embracing this outlook would be unrealistic to expect of those living without adequate shelter or enough food to eat. I personally had two separate moments in my life when I didn't have money for food for several weeks. It was a fearful and anxious time. When one is seriously hungry, there is little room for contented thought.

Aside from that scenario, most of us have lives full of blessings. Our finances might be tighter than we wish. We might need to live simply and shop sales. That doesn't mean the joy of enough can't be found. As I get older, I find it a privilege to wake up each morning to a new day. So many of my former friends and colleagues no longer have that privilege. Others are struggling with health challenges and mobility issues. Each day I try to be grateful for what I have.

Discovering the joy of enough has allowed me to dive deep into what I want for my future. While I am always thoughtful in my spending, and keep my eye on our future needs, I have let go of the need to desperately accumulate wealth. Money has become a tool to use, an asset to barter with and manage effectively, not an end goal in itself. I have seen so many people pass away without ever enjoying the riches they had accumulated. They lived a life of scarcity, ever fearful of not having enough. Then they were gone. I find that incredibly sad.

If you're feeling a weird disconnect as you read this, you are not alone. We are taught in our culture that being content with what we have is not acceptable. The implication is that feeling we have enough will keep us stagnant, never moving from our current status. We will stop reaching for the stars. Not true. Knowing you have enough, that you are enough just as you are, will empower you.

My future is no longer defined by work that simply amasses more wealth. I am at peace with the knowledge our finances will ebb and flow along the way, and that's okay. With dreams no longer driven by living in a state of want—more money, more fame, more achievement, more recognition, more awards—or the pressure of survival, I am motivated simply by my passion for writing, and my desire to be of service to others.

If unexpected expenses arise, no problem. I will simply find a way to spend less and head back to work. If health challenges create limits, I will find a way to continue in spite of them. Each and every day, I will pause and spend some time in gratitude for what I do have. The joy of enough is real and it fills my being.

My hope is you will allow the joy of enough to become a part of your daily life. Make a habit of expressing gratitude for all you do have, and try to spend a few minutes each day affirming you are enough just as you are. The knowledge you have enough will also help you reach confidently for the future and all it has to offer. Change starts with a shift in your relationship with money. Try to root out and release old negative messages you carry, seek out any knowledge you lack, and, if needed, find a professional that can offer support.

The joy of enough is not an end goal, it's a launching point. Now is the time to weed those seeds of scarcity and erase the negative tapes. It's time to be brave and take a leap of faith. It's time to fly. You can do it!

MARILYN R. WILSON

Marilyn is a freelance writer, published author, speaker, and poet with a passion for sharing the stories of others. Her career began in an unusual way—when she answered a Craigslist ad for which she had no qualifications. Somehow she made the cut and quickly discovered a deep passion for hearing others share their unique stories.

Over the next seventeen years she conducted over 200 interviews, was co-owner of a magazine, and was published in others. In 2015 she launched her first book, *Life Outside the Box*, followed in 2018 by *The Wisdom of Listening*.

Whether through a random encounter or a scheduled interview, her goal is the same—to give wings to the stories of inspiring individuals, and to pass on the wisdom shared with her in interviews and discovered during her own life journey.

marilynrwilson.com

@marilynrwilson_official

MarilynRWilsonWriter

@marilynwilson8752

ACKNOWLEDGEMENTS

So many people helped with the creation of this book. My thanks in particular to

- the nine contributing authors who have shared their challenges, insights, and accomplishments within these pages, to help change our world for the better. Your passion to show up and give freely of your knowledge has been outstanding. You are amazing women.
- my Connected Woman community. You have inspired me to keep going when I have faced my own challenges. You were there for me as this project was envisioned and realized. You are my board of directors, my cheerleaders, my friends. For that I am eternally grateful.
- my experts, editor Naomi Pauls and designer Carly Franklin. Without their incredible talents and patience, this book would not have become a reality.
- my family, friends, and colleagues who have been there for me, cheering me on and giving me the support to make this book a reality. Special thanks to my loving and incredibly supportive husband, who has faith in me no matter what I choose to do.

- my mother, from whom I get my determination (some say stubbornness), my wicked sense of humour (some say sarcasm), and my ability to see beyond the obstacles, no matter how insurmountable they may seem (definitely optimism). I hope you're proud of the woman I've become.

I am extremely grateful and blessed to have so many wonderful people in my life. You, dear reader, are one of them.